P9-EMH-992

COMPLETE RUSSIAN

THE BASICS

REVISED & UPDATED

REVISED BY NADYA L. PETERSON, PH.D.

Assistant Professor of Russian

University of Pennsylvania

◆

Based on the original

by Aron Pressman

LIVING LANGUAGE®
A Random House Company

Published in the United States by Living Language, A Random House Company

www.livinglanguage.com

Editor: Zviezdana Verzich
Production Editor: Jacinta O'Halloran
Production Manager: Heather Lanigan

ISBN 1-4000-2153-7

Library of Congress Cataloging-in-Publication Data available upon request.

This book is available for special discounts for bulk purchases for sales promotions or premiums. Special editions, including personalized covers, excerpts of existing books, and corporate imprints, can be created in large quantities for special needs. For more information, write to Special Markets/Premium Sales, 1745 Broadway, MD 6-2, New York, NY, 10019 or e-mail specialmarkets@randomhouse.com.

Printed in the United States of America
10 9 8 7 6 5 4 3 2

CONTENTS

INTRODUCTION

Living Language® Complete Russian: The Basics makes it easy to learn how to speak, read, and write Russian. This course is a thoroughly revised and updated version of *Living Russian, The Complete Living Language Course®*. The same highly effective method of language instruction is still used, but the content has been updated to reflect modern usage, and the format has been clarified. In this course, the basic elements of the language have been carefully selected and condensed into forty short lessons. If you can study about thirty minutes a day, you can master this course and learn to speak Russian in a few weeks.

You'll learn Russian the way you learned English, starting with simple words and progressing to more complex phrases. Just listen and repeat after the native instructors on the recordings. To help you immerse yourself in the language, you'll hear only Russian spoken. Hear it, say it, and absorb it through use and repetition.

This *Living Language® Complete Russian: The Basics* course book provides English translations and brief explanations for each lesson. The first seven lessons cover pronunciation, laying the foundation for learning the vocabulary, phrases, and grammar, which are explained in the later chapters. If you already know a little Russian, you can use the book as a phrase book and reference. In addition to the forty lessons, there is a Summary of Russian Grammar, plus verb conjugations and a section on writing letters.

Also included in the course package is the *Living*

Language® *Russian Dictionary.* It contains more than 15,000 entries, with many of the definitions illustrated by phrases and idiomatic expressions. The most essential words are preceded by an * to make them easy to find. You can increase your vocabulary and range of expression just by browsing through the dictionary.

Practice your Russian as much as possible. Even if you can't manage a trip abroad, watching Russian movies, reading Russian magazines, eating at Russian restaurants, and talking with Russian-speaking friends are enjoyable ways to help reinforce what you have learned with *Living Language® Complete Russian: The Basics.* Now, let's begin.

The following instructions will tell you what to do. Ни пу́ха, ни пера́! Good luck!

COURSE MATERIAL

1. Two 90-minute cassettes or three 60-minute compact discs.

2. *Living Language® Complete Russian: The Basics* course book. This book is designed for use with the recorded lessons, but it may also be used alone as a reference. It contains the following sections:

   Basic Russian in 40 Lessons
   Summary of Russian Grammar
   Verb conjugations
   Letter and E-mail writing
   Internet Resources

3. *Living Language® Russian Dictionary.* The Russian/English–English/Russian dictionary contains more than 15,000 entries. Phrases and idiomatic expressions illustrate many of the definitions. The most essential words are preceded by an *.

INSTRUCTIONS

1. Look at page 2. The words in **boldface** type are the ones you will hear on the recording.

2. Now read Lesson 1 all the way through. Note the points to listen for when you play the recording. The first word you will hear is **Алекса́ндр** (Alexander).

3. Start the recording, listen carefully, and say the words aloud in the pauses provided. Go through the lesson once, and don't worry if you can't pronounce everything correctly the first time around. Try it again and keep repeating the lesson until you are comfortable with it. The more often you listen and repeat, the longer you will remember the material.

4. Now go on to the next lesson. If you take a break between lessons, it's always good to review the previous lesson before starting on a new one.

5. In the manual, there are two kinds of quizzes. With matching quizzes, you must select the English translation of the Russian sentence. The other type requires you to fill in the blanks with the correct Russian word. If you make any mistakes, reread the section.

6. There are 18 supplemental vocabulary sections in the course. Each one focuses on a useful theme that is loosely related to the content of the surrounding lessons. Practice the lists through repetition, self-quizzes, or with flash cards to build a solid foundation in Russian vocabulary.

7. Even after you have finished the forty lessons and achieved a perfect score on the Final Quiz, keep practicing your Russian by listening to the

recordings and speaking with Russian-speaking friends. For further study, try *Ultimate Russian Beginner-Intermediate* and *Ultimate Russian Advanced,* both from the experts at Living Language. Or, go to our website at *www. livinglanguage.com* for more information on the available Russian courses and reference materials.

LESSON 1

A. THE LETTERS AND SOUNDS OF THE RUSSIAN LANGUAGE

Russian pronunciation will be easy once you learn the rules of pronunciation and reading, which hold true with very few exceptions. It is just as easy to say *ah* as it is to say *oh,* or to say *vast* as it is to say *fast.* But if you pronounce *f* where it should be *v,* or *oh* where it should be *ah,* or *eh* where it should be *ee,* you will speak with a foreign accent. Knowing these rules will help you to have a sound picture of the word you are learning and will help you to recognize it when it is spoken by the native; you want to understand as well as to speak!

Russian is *not* phonetic. You *don't* read it the way it is spelled. Many native Russians think they do; most of them are sure they do—they are wrong!

Learn word units. Always try to pronounce pronoun, preposition, and adjective together with the word they modify. Note that all words that have more than one syllable are marked with an accent mark. This is done only for the sake of the student. Accent marks will not be found in reading material outside of textbooks, but for the sake of proper pronunciation, it is necessary to memorize the stress in each word.

Russian punctuation varies little from that of English in the use of the semi-colon, colon, exclamation point, question mark, and period. However, the use of the comma is determined by concrete grammatical rules and generally does not, as in English, indicate a voice stop.

Remember that the Russian language is not phonetic. Most letters represent several sounds. It is important to keep this in mind at the beginning of your study and to acquire the proper speech habits at the very start.

The Russian language has twenty consonant letters representing thirty-five consonant sounds, since fifteen of these twenty letters can represent either soft or hard (palatalized or nonpalatalized) sounds. Three are hard only; two are soft only. There are ten vowels and one semi-vowel.

Softness, or palatalization, of consonants is indicated by the vowels: **е, ё, и, ю, я,** and **ь** (soft sign). When a consonant is followed by one of these vowels, the consonant is palatalized, i.e., it is soft. In palatalization, the articulation of a consonant in its alphabet (nonpalatalized) form is altered in a specific way: the place and manner of articulation remain the same, but the middle part of the speaker's tongue moves up to the palate to produce "palatalization." Palatalization in the Russian language has particular significance and should therefore be carefully studied, as the meaning of a word can be changed through palatalization. Listen carefully and try to imitate.

The alphabet is given in Lesson 3, but listening to the tape and looking at the spelling of the following names and words will help you to recognize the different sounds each letter can represent.

B. NAMES

Many Russian sounds are like English. Listen to and repeat the following Russian names and notice which sounds are similar and which are different:

Алекса́ндр	Alexander
Алексе́й	Alexis

Анто́н	Anthony
Бори́с	Boris
Валенти́н	Valentine
Варва́ра	Barbara
Ви́ктор	Victor
Влади́мир	Vladimir
Воло́дя	Volodya, dim. of Vladimir
Гео́ргий	George
Дави́д	David
Дми́трий	Dimitri
Евге́ний	Eugene
Екатери́на	Catherine
Еле́на	Helen
Елизаве́та	Elizabeth
Же́ня	Gene, dim. of Eugene or Eugenia
Заха́р	Zachary
Ива́н	John, Ivan
И́горь	Igor
Ири́на	Irene
Ка́тя	Kate, dim. of Catherine
Ко́ля	Kolya, dim. of Nicholas
Константи́н	Constantine
Леони́д	Leonid
Ли́за	Liza, dim. of Elizabeth
Любо́вь	Amy
Лю́ба	dim. of Amy
Людми́ла	Ludmilla
Макси́м	Maxim
Маргари́та	Margaret
Михаи́л	Michael
Наде́жда	Nadezhda
На́дя	Nadya, dim. of Nadezhda or Nadine
Ната́лья	Natalie

Ната́ша	Natasha, dim. of Natalie
Никола́й	Nicholas
О́льга	Olga
Па́вел	Paul
Пётр	Peter
Серге́й	Sergei
Фёдор	Theodore

NOTE

1. Each vowel is pronounced clearly, but the same letter does not always have the same sound. This is especially true of the letter *o*, which sometimes has the sound of *oh* but more often the sound of *ah*. The letter *e* sometimes has the sound of *eh* and sometimes the sound of *yeh*.

2. The accent mark (´) shows the syllable that is stressed. The stressed vowel is pronounced in its alphabet form, with more emphasis (slightly longer and louder).

3. Each word has only one stressed syllable.

4. Any syllable can be stressed.

5. All syllables after the stressed syllable are pronounced with less emphasis.

Pay attention to the consonant and its palatalization.

C. GEOGRAPHICAL NAMES

Австра́лия	Australia
А́зия	Asia
Аме́рика	America
Аргенти́на	Argentina
Арха́нгельск	Arkhangelsk
Байка́л	Baikal (Lake)
Баку́	Baku
Болга́рия	Bulgaria
Варша́ва	Warsaw
Вашингто́н	Washington

Великобрита́ния	Great Britain
Владивосто́к	Vladivostok
Во́лга	Volga
Гали́ция	Galicia
Герма́ния	Germany
Гру́зия	Georgia
Днепр	Dnieper
Дуна́й	Danube
Евро́па	Europe
Еги́пет	Egypt
И́ндия	India
Ита́лия	Italy
Ирты́ш	Irtisch (River)
Кавка́з	Caucasus
Калифо́рния	California
Ки́ев	Kiev
Константино́поль	Constantinople
Крым	Crimea
Македо́ния	Macedonia
Ме́ксика	Mexico
Москва́	Moscow
Нева́	Neva
Оде́сса	Odessa
Ока́	Oka
Псков	Pskov
Росси́я	Russia
Ряза́нь	Ryazan
Сама́ра	Samara
Севасто́поль	Sevastopol

LESSON 2

A. COGNATES: WORDS SIMILAR IN RUSSIAN AND ENGLISH

Listen to these Russian words, which are general equivalents of English words. These words are descended from the same root and are called cognates. Note the character of Russian pronunciation as well as Russian intonation.

абсолюти́зм	absolutism
аванга́рд	avant-garde
авиа́ция	aviation
автобиогра́фия	autobiography
атмосфе́ра	atmosphere
бактериоло́гия	bacteriology
балла́да	ballad
баро́метр	barometer
батаре́я	battery
библиогра́фия	bibliography
вака́нсия	vacancy
вандали́зм	vandalism
витами́ны	vitamins
гара́нтия	guarantee
генера́тор	generator
геоло́гия	geology
гладиа́тор	gladiator
дарвини́зм	Darwinism
деклара́ция	declaration
демокра́тия	democracy
диа́гноз	diagnosis
диале́кт	dialect
дие́та	diet
дисципли́на	discipline
жонглёр	juggler

зигза́г	zigzag
игнори́ровать	ignore
иде́я	idea
имита́ция	imitation
индивидуали́зм	individualism
инспе́ктор	inspector
инстру́ктор	instructor
инструме́нт	instrument
калейдоско́п	kaleidoscope
карикату́ра	caricature
компози́тор	composer
коопера́ция	cooperation
корреспонде́нт	correspondent
кри́тика	criticism
лабири́нт	labyrinth
лаборато́рия	laboratory
либерали́зм	liberalism
литерату́ра	literature
маркси́зм	Marxism
медици́на	medicine
мето́дика	method
микроско́п	microscope
негати́в	negative
обсервато́рия	observatory
о́пера	opera
опера́ция	operation
оппози́ция	opposition
оптими́ст	optimist
павильо́н	pavilion
панора́ма	panorama
парази́т	parasite
перспекти́ва	perspective
пикни́к	picnic
пирами́да	pyramid
популя́рный	popular
привиле́гия	privilege

прогре́сс	progress
радиа́тор	radiator
раке́та	rocket
резервуа́р	reservoir
репута́ция	reputation
рефле́ктор	reflector
стати́стика	statistics
та́ктика	tactics
телеско́п	telescope
тео́рия	theory
терминоло́гия	terminology
уверти́ора	overture
университе́т	university
эволю́ция	evolution

B. GEOGRAPHICAL NAMES II

Алжи́р	Algeria
А́встрия	Austria
А́нглия	England
Бе́льгия	Belgium
Брази́лия	Brazil
Гре́ция	Greece
Да́ния	Denmark
Изра́иль	Israel
Ирла́ндия	Ireland
Испа́ния	Spain
Кана́да	Canada
Кита́й	China
Коре́я	Korea
Люксембу́рг	Luxembourg
Маро́кко	Morocco
Нидерла́нды	Netherlands
Но́вая Зела́ндия	New Zealand
Норве́гия	Norway
Португа́лия	Portugal

Таила́нд	Thailand
Ту́рция	Turkey
Швейца́рия	Switzerland
Шве́ция	Sweden
Шотла́ндия	Scotland
Япо́ния	Japan

LESSON 3

A. INTRODUCTION TO THE RUSSIAN ALPHABET

Russian uses the Cyrillic alphabet, which derives from the Greek, whereas English is written with the Latin alphabet. However, there are a few letters that are shared by both languages. Still other letters may be familiar to you from basic mathematics and the names of college fraternities and sororities. As you use this book, you will quickly become familiar with the different letters and sounds, and soon you'll be able to recognize them instantly.

B. THE ALPHABET

RUSSIAN	LETTER SCRIPT		NAME
Аа	_A_	_a_	ah
Бб	_Б_	_б_	beh
Вв	_B_	_в_	veh
Гг	_Г_	_г_	geh
Дд	_D_	_д_	deh
Ее	_E_	_e_	yeh
Ёё	_Ë_	_ë_	yoh
Жж	_Ж_	_ж_	zheh

Зз	З	з	zeh
Ии	И	и	ee
Йй	Й	й	y (i short)
Кк	К	к	kah
Лл	Л	л	ell
Мм	М	м	em
Нн	Н	н	en
Оо	О	о	oh
Пп	П	п	peh
Рр	Р	р	err
Сс	С	с	ess
Тт	Т	т	teh
Уу	У	у	ooh
Фф	Ф	ф	eff
Хх	Х	х	khah
Цц	Ц	ц	tseh
Чч	Ч	ч	cheh
Шш	Ш	ш	shah
Щщ	Щ	щ	shchah
Ыы	Ы	ы	ih
Ьь		ь	soft sign
Ъъ		ъ	hard sign
Ээ	Э	э	eh
Юю	Ю	ю	yoo
Яя	Я	я	yah

LESSON 4

A. Palatalized and Nonpalatalized Syllables

Here are all possible combinations of consonants followed by vowels. On the tape, each hard syllable is followed by the palatalized or soft syllable. Listen carefully and try to hear the difference. Imitate. Listen again. Try to hear the difference in your own pronunciation.

ба ва га да жа за ка ла ма на па ра са та фа ха ца ча ша ща

бя вя гя* дя зя кя* ля мя ня пя ря ся тя фя

бо во го до жо зо ко ло мо но по ро со то фо хо цо чо шо що

бё вё гё* дё жё зё кё* лё мё нё пё рё сё тё фё чё шё щё

бу ву гу ду жу зу ку лу му ну пу ру су ту фу ху цу чу шу щу

бю вю дю жю** зю кю* лю мю ню пю рю сю тю фю хю*

бэ вэ гэ дэ зэ кэ лэ мэ нэ пэ рэ сэ тэ фэ хэ цэ

бе ве ге де же зе ке ле ме не пе ре се те фе хе це че ше ще

---

* Possible only in words of foreign origin.
** Pronounced soft (palatalized), as in жюри (jury), a word of foreign origin.

бы вы ды зы лы мы ны пы ры сы ты фы хы цы

би ви ги ди жи зи ки ли ми ни пи ри си ти фи хи
ци чи ши щи

NOTE

Keep in mind the following points:

жо and жё }	are pronounced alike.
цэ and це	
цы and ци	the letters ж, ц, ш
шо and шё	are always hard.
чо and чё	the letters ч and щ are
що and щё	always soft.

LESSON 5

A. VOWELS

1. The letter A
   a. When stressed, it is pronounced like the English *ah*:

а́рмия	army
ла́мпа	lamp
ма́ло	little

   b. When unstressed, before a stressed syllable, it is pronounced *ah,* but shorter.

команди́р	commander
каде́т	cadet

   c. In most other positions it is given a neuter sound—i.e., like that of the letter *a* in *sofa*:

каранда́ш	pencil
магази́н	store
аванга́рд	avant-garde

2. The letter O
   a. When stressed, it is pronounced *oh*, as in *lawn*:

| он | he |
| до́брый | pleasant |

   b. When unstressed, it is either in first place before the stressed syllable or used initially and is pronounced *ah*:

Бори́с	Boris
она́	she
оно́	it
отвеча́ть	to answer

   c. In all other positions it is given a neuter sound—i.e., like the *a* in *sofa*:

хорошо́	well
пло́хо	badly
молоко́	milk

3. The letter **У**
   is pronounced both stressed and unstressed like the English *ooh*:

стул	chair
суп	soup
у́тро	morning
туда́	there (in that direction)
уро́к	lesson
узнава́ть	to find out
учи́тель	teacher

4. The letter **Ы**
   has no strict equivalent in English; however, it
   closely resembles the *i* sound in *sit*:

ты	you
мы	we
вы	you *(pl.)*
мы́ло	soap
малы́	small (predicative form)
столы́	tables
была́	she was

5. The letter **Э**
   is pronounced like the *eh* in *echo*:

э́то	this
э́ти	these
поэ́т	poet
эта́п	stage

NOTE

The function of the following vowels—**е, ё, и, ю, я**—which are
preceded by a glide (the sound similar to the final sound in the
English word *may*) is the palatalization of the preceding consonant,
to which they lose the above-mentioned glide. However, when they
follow a vowel or soft or hard signs, or when they appear initially,
they are pronounced as in the alphabet—i.e., with an initial glide.

6. The letter **И**
   always palatalizes the preceding consonant and
   is pronounced like the *ee* in *beet* except after the
   letters **ж, ц, ш,** which are never palatalized; then
   и is pronounced like the Russian sound **ы**:

си́ла	strength
Ли́за	Liza

никогда́	never
иногда́	sometimes
ши́на[1]	tire
жить[1]	live

7. The letter **Й**

 a. It is never stressed. It is pronounced like the final sound in the English word *boy*:

мой	my
пойти́	to go
споко́йно	quietly

 b. It is very seldom used initially, except in some words of foreign origin:

| **Нью-Йорк** | New York |

8. The letter **Е**

 a. It always palatalizes the preceding consonant, except the letters **ж, ц, ш.** When stressed, it is pronounced like the *yeh* in *yet*:

нет	no, not
Ве́ра	Vera, faith
сесть	to sit down

 b. In unstressed positions it is pronounced like the soft *i* in *sit*:

всегда́	always
сестра́	sister
жена́	wife

---

[1] Here **и** is pronounced **ы** because **ж** and **ш** are never palatalized.

c. Initially, or after another vowel, it is pronounced with the glide stressed, like *yeh,* or unstressed, like *yeeh*:

ей	to her
её	her
пое́здка	trip

9. The letter **Ё**
   always palatalizes the preceding consonant and is always stressed. It is pronounced like the *yo* in *yoke*:

мёд	honey
тётя	aunt
ёлка	fir tree
моё	my (*n*)
ещё	yet, still

10. The letter **Я**
    a. It always palatalizes the preceding consonant. When stressed in the middle of the word, it is pronounced *yah;* when unstressed, it is pronounced either like the short *i* of *sit* or like the neutral *a* of *sofa* if it is the last letter of a word:

мя́со	meat
мая́к	lighthouse
тётя	aunt
де́сять	ten

    b. When used initially, it retains its glide; when stressed, it is pronounced *yah;* when unstressed, *yih*:

я́блоко	apple
янва́рь	January
язы́к	language, tongue

11. The letter **Ю**
    a. It always palatalizes the preceding consonant. It is pronounced *ooh* in the body of the word:

    | **Лю́ба** | Lyuba |
    | **люблю́** | I love |
    | **люби́ть** | to love |

    b. When used initially, it retains its glide and is pronounced *yooh*:

    | **ю́бка** | skirt |
    | **юбиле́й** | jubilee |

12. The letter **Ь**
    is called the "soft" sign; it palatalizes the preceding consonant, allowing the following vowel to retain its glide. It also indicates that the preceding consonant is soft when written at the end of a word:

    | **пье́са** | play |
    | **пья́ный** | drunk |
    | **свинья́** | pig |

13. The letter **Ъ**
    is called the "hard" sign. It indicates that the preceding consonant remains hard and that the following vowel retains its glide:

    | **объём** | volume |
    | **объясня́ть** | explain |

LESSON 6

A. CONSONANTS

Russian consonants, like those in every language, may be voiced or voiceless. The distinction between voiced and voiceless consonants is based on one aspect of otherwise identical articulation: in voiced consonants vocal cords are involved in articulation, while in voiceless consonants they are not. The pairs are:

б в г д ж з	(voiced)	b v g d zh z
п ф к т ш с	(voiceless)	p f k t sh s

When two consonants are pronounced together, both must be either voiced or voiceless. In Russian, the second one always remains as it is and the first one changes accordingly.

всё, все, вчера́	**в**=v, pronounced *f*
сде́лать, сдать	**с**=s, pronounced *z*

The preposition в (in) is very often pronounced *f*. В шко́ле (in school) is pronounced *fshkoh-leh*.

Russian consonants can also be soft or hard, i.e., palatalized or nonpalatalized, when followed by the letters е, ё, и, ю, я or ь; exceptions are the consonants ж, ш, ц, which are always hard.

This looks complicated, but it is much easier to learn this in the beginning and to begin speaking correctly than it is to try to correct erroneous pronunciation later on. Listen carefully and try to hear the above-mentioned differences.

Б

1. Pronounced like the *b* in *bread*:

брат	brother
бума́га	paper
бага́ж	baggage

2. Palatalized:

бе́лый	white
бино́кль	binoculars

3. Voiceless, like the *p* at the end of a word or before a voiceless consonant:

ю́бка	skirt
зуб	tooth
хлеб	bread

4. Voiceless palatalized:

дробь	buckshot
зыбь	ripple

В

1. Pronounced like the *v* in *very*:

ваш	your
вот	here
вода́	water

2. Palatalized:

ве́ра	faith
конве́рт	envelope
весь	all

3. Voiceless, like the *f* at the end of a word or before a voiceless consonant:

Ки́ев	Kiev
в шко́ле	in school
вчера́	yesterday
кров	shelter

4. Voiceless palatalized:

кровь	blood

Г

1. Pronounced like the *g* in *good*:

газе́та	newspaper
где	where
гармо́ния	harmony

2. Palatalized:

гита́ра	guitar
геоме́трия	geometry

3. Like the Russian **x** before **к**:

легко́	lightly, easily
мя́гко	softly

4. Like the *v* in the genitive ending, masculine and neuter:

его́	his
ничего́	nothing
сего́дня	today

5. Voiceless, like the *k* at the end of a word:

рог	horn
четве́рг	Thursday

Д

1. Pronounced like the *d* in *door*:

дом	house
родно́й	kindred

2. Palatalized:

де́рево	wood
оди́н	one

3. Voiceless, like the *t* at the end of a word or before a voiceless consonant:

обе́д	dinner
подко́ва	horseshoe
по́дпись	signature

4. Voiceless palatalized:

грудь	breast

Ж

1. Pronounced like the *s* in *measure*: always hard:

жар	heat
жена́	wife
жить	to live
пожа́р	fire

2. Voiceless, like the *sh* at the end of a word or before a voiceless consonant:

ло́жка	spoon
муж	husband

З

1. Pronounced like the *z* in *zebra*:

зда́ние	building
зна́ть	to know

2. Palatalized:

зелёный	green
зима́	winter

3. Voiceless, like the *s* at the end of a word or before a voiceless consonant:

ползти́	crawl
воз	cart

К

1. Pronounced like the *k* in *kept*:

кни́га	book
класс	class
каранда́ш	pencil

2. Palatalized:

ке́пка	cap
кероси́н	kerosene
Ки́ев	Kiev
кино́	movie

3. Voiced, like the *g* in *good,* before a voiced consonant:

вокза́л	railroad station
экза́мен	examination
к бра́ту	to the brother

Л

1. Pronounced like the *l* in *look*:

ло́жка	spoon
ла́мпа	lamp
мел	chalk

2. Palatalized:

любо́вь	love
лёгкий	light
мель	shoal
боль	pain

LESSON 7

A. CONSONANTS II

М

1. Pronounced like the *m* in *man*:

ма́ма	mama
магни́т	magnet
дом	house
паро́м	ferry

2. Palatalized:

мя́со	meat
ми́на	mine

Н

1. Pronounced like the *n* in *noon*:

нос	nose
нож	knife
балко́н	balcony

2. Palatalized:

не́бо	sky
неде́ля	week
ня́ня	nurse
ко́нь	horse

П

1. Palatalized:

пе́рвый	first
письмо́	letter
цепь	chain

Р

1. Pronounced like the *r* in *root*:

ру́сский	Russian
пара́д	parade
пода́рок	gift
рука́	hand

2. Palatalized:

рис	rice
поря́док	order
дверь	door

С

1. Pronounced like the *s* in *see*:

сон	dream
суп	soup
свет	light
мя́со	meat
ма́сло	butter

2. Palatalized:

се́вер	north
село́	village
весь	all

3. Voiced, like the *z* before a voiced consonant:

сде́лать	to do
сгоре́ть	to burn down

Т

1. Pronounced like the *t* in *table*:

таба́к	tobacco
тот	that
стол	table
тогда́	then

2. Palatalized:

тень	shade
стена́	wall

3. Voiced like the *d* before a voiced consonant:

отда́ть	to give away
отгада́ть	to guess

Ф

1. Pronounced like the *f* in *friend*:

фа́брика	factory
Фра́нция	France
фарфо́р	porcelain

2. Palatalized:

афи́ша	poster

3. Voiced, like the *v* before a voiced consonant:

афга́нец	Afghan

X

1. Pronounced like the *kh* in *loch*:

ти́хо	quietly
хорошо́	well
те́хника	technique
блоха́	flea

2. Palatalized

хи́на	quinine
хи́мия	chemistry

Ц

Pronounced like the *ts* in *gets;* always hard:

цвето́к	flower
цепь	chain
цирк	circus
пацие́нт	patient (*n.*)
пе́рец	pepper

Ч

1. Pronounced like the *ch* in *church;* always soft:

чай	tea
час	hour
ча́сто	often
чемода́н	suitcase

2. Sometimes pronounced like the *sh* in *shall*:

что	what
коне́чно	of course

Ш

Pronounced like the *sh* in *shall;* always hard:

шаг за ша́гом	step after step
ша́хматы	chess
ши́на	tire
шёлк	silk
шерсть	wool
ты говори́шь	you speak *(sing.)*

Щ

Pronounced like the *shch* in the word combination *fresh cheese;* always soft:

щека́	cheek
щётка	brush
по́мощь	help
посеще́ние	visit

This completes the rules for pronunciation and reading. Read these rules over and over again. Listen to the tapes several times. You have learned them not when you have read and understood the rules, but when you can remember and repeat the sounds and words correctly without looking at the book. Master these, and you will speak Russian well.

FIVE FUNDAMENTAL RULES

1. Remember which syllable is stressed.
2. Remember that unstressed o is pronounced *ah* in prestressed position.
3. Remember that when two consonants are next to each other, the first changes according to the second.
4. Remember that unstressed e is pronounced *ih*.
5. Remember that the letters e, ё, и, ю, я, and ь palatalize the preceding consonant unless it has no palatalized counterpart.

LESSON 8

A. MASCULINE, FEMININE, NEUTER, PLURAL

All Russian nouns, pronouns, adjectives, and ordinal numbers, as well as some cardinal numbers and even several verb forms, have gender: masculine, feminine, or neuter. In the plural there is only one form for all genders.

1. Most nouns, pronouns, and past tense forms of verbs end in:

MASCULINE	FEMININE	NEUTER	PLURAL
hard consonant	a, я	o, e	a, ы, и

2. Most adjectives, ordinal numbers, and participles end in:

MASCULINE	FEMININE	NEUTER	PLURAL
ой, ый, ий	ая, яя	ое, ее	ые, ие
он	она́	оно́	они́
he	she	it	they
мой	моя́	моё	мои́
my	my	my	my
мой брат	моя́ сестра́	моё окно́	мои́ де́ти
my brother	my sister	my window	my children
твой	твоя́	твоё	твои́
your (sing., fam.)	your	your	your
твой	твоя́	твоё	твои́
каранда́ш	кни́га	пальто́	де́ньги
your pencil	your book	your coat	your money
наш дом	на́ша	на́ше	на́ши
	кварти́ра	село́	кни́ги
our house	our	our	our books
	apartment	village	
ваш	ва́ша	ва́ше	ва́ши
your (pl., polite)	your	your	your
ваш стул	ва́ша ла́мпа	ва́ше по́ле	ва́ши
			руба́шки
your chair	your lamp	your field	your shirts
э́тот	э́та	э́то	э́ти
this	this	this	these
бе́лый	бе́лая	бе́лое	бе́лые
white	white	white	white
Э́тот стол	Э́та стена́	Э́то пла́тье	Э́ти сте́ны
бе́лый.	бе́лая.	бе́лое.	бе́лые.
This table is	This wall	This dress	These walls
white.	is white.	is white.	are white.
большо́й	больша́я	большо́е	больши́е
large	large	large	large
его́	её	его́	их
his	her	its	their
его́ оте́ц	её оте́ц		их оте́ц
his father	her father		their father
чей оте́ц	чья мать	чьё окно́	чьи кни́ги
whose	whose	whose	whose books
father	mother	window	
свой	своя́	своё	свои́
one's own	one's own	one's own	one's own

кра́сный	кра́сная	кра́сное	кра́сные
red	red	red	red
чёрный	чёрная	чёрное	чёрные
black	black	black	black
си́ний	си́няя	си́нее	си́ние
blue	blue	blue	blue
оди́н	одна́	одно́	одни́
one	one	one	alone, only
два	две	два	
two	two	two	
пе́рвый	пе́рвая	пе́рвое	пе́рвые
first	first	first	first
второ́й	втора́я	второ́е	вторы́е
second	second	second	second
тре́тий	тре́тья	тре́тье	тре́тьи
third	third	third	third

NOTE

Pronouns, adjectives, and ordinal numbers always agree in gender with the nouns they modify.

QUIZ 1

Match the Russian words with the correct English translations.

1. оди́н		a. this (m.)
2. кра́сная		b. my children
3. де́ньги		c. This wall is white.
4. он		d. our books
5. ва́ша ла́мпа		e. her
6. Э́та стена́ бе́лая.		f. he
7. э́тот		g. first (f.)
8. на́ши кни́ги		h. red (f.)
9. мои́ де́ти		i. children
10. мой брат		j. one (m.)
11. её		k. these
12. де́ти		l. money
13. пе́рвая		m. your field
14. ва́ше по́ле		n. your lamp
15. э́ти		o. my sister
16. моя́ сестра́		p. my brother

ANSWERS

1—j; 2—h; 3—l; 4—f; 5—n; 6—c; 7—a; 8—d; 9—b; 10—p; 11—e; 12—i; 13—g; 14—m; 15—k; 16—o.

LESSON 9

A. CHARACTERISTICS OF THE CASES

With few exceptions, all nouns, pronouns, and adjectives decline. Each declension has six cases used to answer the following question words in their respective case forms (some preceded by the appropriate prepositions):

CASE	QUESTIONS
Nominative (subject):	**Кто? Что?** Who? What?
Genitive (possession, negation):	**Кого? Чего?** Whom? What? **От кого? От чего?** From whom? From what? **У кого? У чего?** At/by whom? At/by what? **Без кого? Без чего?** Without whom? Without what?
Dative (indirect object):	**Кому? Чему?** To whom? To what? **К кому? К чему?** Toward whom? Toward what?
Accusative (direct object):	**Кого? Что?** Whom? What? **Куда?** Where (direction toward)?

Instrumental (object as an instrument, manner of action):	**Кем? Чем?** By whom? By what? **С кем? С чем?** With whom? With what?
Prepositional or Locative (location, also with certain prepositions):	**О ком? О чём?** About whom? About what? **В ком? В чём?** In whom? In what? **Где?** Where?

1. The nominative case supplies the subject of the sentence.

2. The genitive is the case of possession and is also used with many prepositions, the most common of which are без (without), для (for), до (up to), из (out of), около (near by, about), от (from), после (after), and у (at or by).

3. The dative case is used in the meaning of "to whom." Prepositions governing the dative case are к (to) and по (along).

4. The accusative is the direct-object case. Prepositions used with this case include в (to, into), за (behind), and на (to, into, on) in the sense of direction.

5. The instrumental case indicates the manner of action or the instrument with which the action is performed. Prepositions governing the instrumental case include между (between), перед (in front of), and с (with).

6. The prepositional or locative case indicates location, but it is also used when speaking about something or someone. The prepositions most frequently used with this case are в (in), на (on), о (about), and при (in the presence of).

B.   WORD STUDY

звони́ть-позвони́ть*	to call (on the phone)
почему́	why
вме́сте	together
потому́ что	because
говори́ть-сказа́ть	to say
уже́	already
непра́вильно	incorrectly
ка́ждый	each, every
зада́ча	problem, task

LESSON 10

A.   Кто (Who?) and Никто́ (No One)

NOTE

When used with prepositions, the negative expression никто́ splits into three words: the negative particle ни, the preposition, and the declined form of кто. (Никто́ is used only with negated verbs.) This will be clear after you study these phrases.

* This pair of verbs represents an aspectual pair of verbs, a characteristic of Russian which will be discussed later.

NOMINATIVE:

Кто он?	Who is he?
Кто она?	Who is she?
Кто они?	Who are they?
Кто это сделал?	Who did this?
Кто сказал это?	Who said this?

NEGATIVE:

Никто не сделал.	No one did this.
Никто не сказал.	No one said it.

GENITIVE:

Кого нет дома?	Who is not at home?
Ч кого он живёт?	At whose place (by whom) does he live?
Для кого это?	For whom is that?

NEGATIVE:

Никого нет дома.	No one is at home.
Это ни для кого.	This is for no one.
Не у кого жить.	There is no one to live with (at).

DATIVE:

Кому вы это сказали?	To whom did you say that?
Кому вы дали мою книгу?	To whom did you give my book?
К кому вы идёте?	To whom (whose home) are you going?
Кому здесь холодно?	Who is cold here? (To whom is it cold?)

NEGATIVE:

Не говорите никому.	Don't tell anyone.
Он никому не пишет.	He doesn't write anyone.

ACCUSATIVE:

Кого вы знаете здесь?	Whom do you know here?

На кого она похожа?	Whom does she look like?

NEGATIVE:

Я здесь никого не знаю.	I don't know anyone here.
Не на кого положиться.	Nobody to rely on.

INSTRUMENTAL:

С кем вы были в театре вчера?	With whom were you at the theater yesterday?
Кем вы хотите быть?	What do you want to be?

NEGATIVE:

Я ни с кем не был в театре.	I was with no one at the theater.
Не с кем поговорить.	Nobody to talk to.

LOCATIVE/PREPOSITIONAL:

О ком вы говорите?	Whom are you talking about?
На ком он женат?	To whom is he married?

NEGATIVE:

Мы ни о ком не говорим.	We are not talking about anyone.
Он ни на ком не женат.	He is not married to anyone.

QUIZ 2

Fill in the blanks with the proper form of **кто**.

1.	_____ сказал это?	Who said it?
2.	_____ нет дома?	Who isn't at home?
3.	_____ здесь холодно?	Who is cold here?

4. _____ вы да́ли мою́   To whom did you give my
      кни́гу?   book?
5. _____ вы хоти́те быть?   What do you want to be?
6. На _____ он жена́т?   To whom is he married?
7. Он ни с _____ не   He doesn't talk to anyone.
      говори́т.
8. _____ вы зна́ете здесь?   Whom do you know here?
9. Я _____ здесь не зна́ю.   I don't know anyone here.
10. О _____ вы говори́те?   Whom are you talking about?

ANSWERS

1. Кто 2. Кого́ 3. Кому́ 4. Кому́ 5. Кем 6. ком 7. кем 8. Кого́
9. никого́ 10. ком.

SUPPLEMENTAL VOCABULARY 1: PEOPLE

person	челове́к (m.), лю́ди (nom., pl.)
man	челове́к (m.), мужчи́на (m.)
woman	же́нщина (f.)
adult	взро́слый (m.)
child	ребёнок (m.)
children	де́ти (nom., pl.)
boy	ма́льчик (m.)
girl	де́вочка (f.)
teenager	подро́сток (m.), подро́стки (nom., pl.)
tall/short	высо́кий/ни́зкий
old/young	ста́рый/молодо́й
fat/thin	то́лстый/худо́й
friendly/unfriendly	дружелю́бный/не дружелю́бный
happy/sad	счастли́вый, весёлый/ гру́стный
beautiful/ugly	краси́вый, прекра́сный/ уро́дливый

sick/healthy	больной/здоровый
strong/weak	сильный/слабый
famous	знаменитый
intelligent	умный
talented	талантливый

B. Что? (What?) and Ничего́/Не́чего (Nothing)

NOTE

As with никто́, when used with prepositions, the negative expressions ничего́/не́чего split into three words: the particle ни/не, the preposition, and the declined form of что (чего́ in ничего́/не́чего is the genitive form of что).

NOMINATIVE:

Что э́то?	What is it?
Что там?	What's there?
Я не зна́ю, что э́то.	I don't know what it is.
Что э́то тако́е?	What is this?
Что э́то за зда́ние?	What kind of a building is this?
Что но́вого?	What's new?
Что зна́чит э́то сло́во?	What does this word mean?
Что он сказа́л?	What did he say?

SET EXPRESSION:

| **Ни за что на све́те!** | Not for anything in the world! |

GENITIVE:

| **Для чего́ э́то?** | What's this for? |
| **Чего́ то́лько нет в э́том магази́не!** | What they don't have in this store! |

От чего́ у меня́ боли́т голова́?	Why [what from] does my head ache?

NEGATIVE:

Он ничего́ не сказа́л.	He didn't say anything.
В э́том магази́не ничего́ нет.	There is nothing in this store.
Не́чего беспоко́иться.	Don't you worry! (rude).

SET EXPRESSION:

Посмотри́те, до чего́ э́то дошло́.	Look what it has come to.
Чего́ он то́лько не ви́дел!	What hasn't he seen!

DATIVE:

Чему́ вы удивля́етесь?	What are you surprised at?
К чему́ всё э́то?	What's all this for?

NEGATIVE:

Э́то ни к чему́.	This is unnecessary [for nothing].
Не́чему удивля́ться.	Nothing to be surprised at.

SET EXPRESSION:

Чему́ быть—того́ не минова́ть.	What's to be, will be.

ACCUSATIVE:

Что вы хоти́те посмотре́ть?	What would you like to see?

NEGATIVE:

Не на что жить.	Nothing to live on.

INSTRUMENTAL:

Чем вы пи́шете?	What are you writing with?

| **Заче́м вы пришли́?** | Why [what for] did you come? |

NEGATIVE:

| **Она́ меня́ ниче́м не мо́жет удиви́ть.** | She cannot surprise me with anything. |

LOCATIVE/PREPOSITIONAL:

| **О чём вы говори́те?** | What are you talking about? |
| **При чём тут я?** | What do I have to do with it? |

NEGATIVE:

| **Я ни о чём не говорю́.** | I am not talking about anything. |
| **Не о чём сейча́с писа́ть.** | There is nothing to write about now. |

SET EXPRESSION:

| **В чём де́ло?** | What's the matter? |

C. DECLENSIONS OF NOUNS, ADJECTIVES, AND PRONOUNS

Here are the basic forms of declensions of nouns, adjectives, and pronouns.

Do not try to learn these forms. It is better to remember sentences as you continue with the tapes. As you learn sentences, you can refer to these tables to find out to which group the new words belong.

Grammar is a description of a language, not a set of rules by which a language should abide. Grammar describes many different groups in the language and many exceptions to these groups. The more groups and the more exceptions there are, the richer the language.

1. Nouns

	MASCULINE SINGULAR			
	HARD		SOFT	
	ANIMATE	INANIMATE	ANIMATE	INANIMATE
	STUDENT	QUESTION	INHABITANT	SHED
Nom.	студе́нт	вопро́с	жи́тель	сара́-й
Gen.	студе́нт-а	вопро́с-а	жи́тел-я	сара́-я
Dat.	студе́нт-у	вопро́с-у	жи́тел-ю	сара́-ю
Acc.	студе́нт-а	вопро́с	жи́тел-я	сара́-й
Inst.	студе́нт-ом	вопро́с-ом	жи́тел-ем	сара́-ем
Prep.	о студе́нт-е	о вопро́с-е	о жи́тел-е	о сара́-е

	MASCULINE PLURAL			
Nom.	студе́нт-ы	вопро́с-ы	жи́тел-и	сара́-и
Gen.	студе́нт-ов	вопро́с-ов	жи́тел-ей	сара́-ев
Dat.	студе́нт-ам	вопро́с-ам	жи́тел-ям	сара́-ям
Acc.	студе́нт-ов	вопро́с-ы	жи́тел-ей	сара́-и
Inst.	студе́нт-ами	вопро́с-ами	жи́тел-ями	сара́-ями
Prep.	о студе́нт-ах	о вопро́с-ах	о жи́тел-ях	о сара́-ях

NOTE

The accusative case of animate masculine nouns is the same as the genitive, while the accusative of inanimate masculine nouns is the same as the nominative.

	FEMININE SINGULAR		
	HARD	SOFT	
	ROOM	EARTH	FAMILY
Nom.	ко́мната	земля́	семья́
Gen.	ко́мнат-ы	земл-и́	семь-и́
Dat.	ко́мнат-е	земл-е́	семь-е́
Acc.	ко́мнат-у	зе́мл-ю	семь-ю́
Inst.	ко́мнат-ой(ою)[1]	земл-ёй	семь-ёй
Prep.	о ко́мнат-е	о земл-е́	о семь-е́

[1] ою is a variant used in songs, poems and some dialects.

	FEMININE PLURAL		
Nom.	ко́мнат-ы	зе́мл-и	се́мь-и
Gen.	ко́мнат	земе́л-ь	сем-е́й
Dat.	ко́мнат-ам	зе́мл-ям	се́мь-ям
Acc.	ко́мнат-ы	зе́мл-и	се́мь-и
Inst.	ко́мнат-ами	зе́мл-ями	се́мь-ями
Prep.	о ко́мнат-ах	о зе́мл-ях	о се́мь-ях

	NEUTER SINGULAR		
	HARD	SOFT	
	WINDOW	SEA	WISH
Nom.	окно́	мо́ре	жела́ние
Gen.	окн-а́	мо́р-я	жела́н-ия
Dat.	окн-у́	мо́р-ю	жела́н-ию
Acc.	окн-о́	мо́р-е	жела́н-ие
Inst.	окн-о́м	мо́р-ем	жела́н-ием
Prep.	об[1] окн-е́	о мо́р-е	о жела́н-ии

	NEUTER PLURAL		
Nom.	о́кн-а	мор-я́	жела́н-ия
Gen.	о́к-он	мор-е́й	жела́н-ий
Dat.	о́кн-ам	мор-я́м	жела́н-иям
Acc.	о́кн-а	мор-я́	жела́н-ия
Inst.	о́кн-ами	мор-я́ми	жела́н-иями
Prep.	об[2] о́кн-ах	о мор-я́х	о жела́н-иях

[1,2] **б** is added to the preposition here for the sake of euphony.

2. Some Irregular Declensions

	SINGULAR		
	MASC.	FEM.	NEUT.
	ROAD	MOTHER	NAME
Nom.	путь	мать	и́мя
Gen.	пут-и́	ма́т-ери	и́м-ени
Dat.	пут-и́	ма́т-ери	и́м-ени
Acc.	путь	мать	и́мя
Inst.	пут-ём	ма́т-ерью	и́м-енем
Prep.	о пут-и́	о ма́т-ери	об и́м-ени

	PLURAL			
Nom	пут-и́	ма́т-ери	име-на́	де́т-и
Gen.	пут-е́й	мат-ере́й	им-ён	дет-е́й
Dat.	пут-я́м	мат-еря́м	им-ена́м	де́т-ям
Acc.	пут-и́	мат-ере́й[1]	им-ена́	дет-е́й[1]
Inst.	пут-я́ми	мат-еря́ми	им-ена́ми	дет-ьми́
Prep.	о пут-я́х	о мат-еря́х	об им-ена́х	о де́т-ях

3. Adjectives

	SINGULAR		
	NEW		
	MASC.	FEM.	NEUT.
	ый	ая	ое
Nom.	но́вый	но́вая	но́вое
Gen.	но́в-ого	но́в-ой	но́в-ого
Dat.	но́в-ому	но́в-ой	но́в-ому
Acc.	same as nom. or gen.	но́в-ую	но́в-ое
Inst.	но́в-ым	но́в-ой(ою)	но́в-ым
Prep.	о но́в-ом	о но́в-ой	о но́в-ом

[1] The accusative plural of animate neuter nouns and most feminine nouns is the same as the genitive plural.

	DEAR		
	ой	ая	ое
Nom.	дорогóй	дорогáя	дорогóе
Gen.	дорог-óго	дорог-óй	дорог-óго
Dat.	дорог-óму	дорог-óй	дорог-óму
Acc.	same as nom. or gen.	дорог-ýю	дорог-óе
Inst.	дорог-и́м	дорог-óй(-óю)	дорог-и́м
Prep.	о дорог-óм	о дорог-óй	о дорог-óм

	PLURAL	
	ALL GENDERS	
Nom.	нóв-ые	дорог-и́е
Gen.	нóв-ых	дорог-и́х
Dat.	нóв-ым	дорог-и́м
Acc.	same as nom. or gen.	same as nom. or gen.
Inst.	нóв-ыми	дорог-и́ми
Prep.	о нóв-ых	о дорог-и́х

	BLUE			
	SINGULAR			PLURAL
	MASC.	FEM.	NEUT.	ALL GENDERS
	ий	яя	ее	ие
Nom.	си́н-ий	си́н-яя	си́н-ее	си́н-ие
Gen.	си́н-его	си́н-ей	си́н-его	си́н-их
Dat.	си́н-ему	си́н-ей	си́н-ему	си́н-им
Acc.	same as nom. or gen.	си́н-юю	си́н-ее	same as nom. or gen.
Inst.	си́н-им	си́н-ей(-ею)	си́н-им	си́н-ими
Prep.	о си́н-ем	о си́н-ей	о си́н-ем	о си́н-их

4. PRONOUNS

	SINGULAR				
	1ST PERSON	2ND PERSON	3RD PERSON		
			MASC.	NEUT.	FEM.
Nom.	я	ты	он	оно́	она́
Gen.	меня́	тебя́	его́	его́	её
Dat.	мне	тебе́	ему́	ему́	ей
Acc.	меня́	тебя́	его́	его́	её
Instr.	мной(-о́ю)	тобо́й(-о́ю)	им	им	ей, е́ю
Prep.	обо мне́	о тебе́	о нём	о нём	о ней

	PLURAL		
	1ST PERSON	2ND PERSON	3RD PERSON
Nom.	мы	вы	они́
Gen.	нас	вас	их
Dat.	нам	вам	им
Acc.	нас	вас	их
Instr.	на́ми	ва́ми	и́ми
Prep.	о нас	о вас	о них

REFLEXIVE PRONOUN
SING. OR PLURAL
—
себя́
себе́
себя́
собо́й(-о́ю)
о себе́

	MY			
	SINGULAR			PLURAL
	MASC.	FEM.	NEUTER	ALL GENDERS
Nom.	мой	моя́	моё	мои́
Gen.	моего́	мое́й	моего́	мои́х
Dat.	моему́	мое́й	моему́	мои́м
Acc.	same as nom. or gen.	мою́	моё	same as nom. or gen.
Inst.	мои́м	мое́й(-е́ю)	мои́м	мои́ми
Prep.	о моём	о мое́й	о моём	о мои́х

NOTE

Твой (your, *sing.*), свой (one's own, their own) are declined in the same way as мой.

In expressing the possessive in the third person, the genitive case of the pronouns он, она́, оно́, они́—его́ (his), её (hers), его́ (its), их (theirs)—is used. These pronouns always agree with the gender and number of the possessor.

Их дом хоро́ший.	Their house is nice.
Я ви́дела их дочь.	I saw their daughter.
Он взял её кни́ги.	He took her books.
Его́ кни́га бо́лее интере́сная.	His book is more interesting.

OUR			
	SINGULAR		PLURAL
MASC.	FEM.	NEUTER	ALL GENDERS
Nom. наш	на́ша	на́ше	на́ши
Gen. наш-его	на́ш-ей	на́ш-его	на́ш-их
Dat. наш-ему	на́ш-ей	на́ш-ему	на́ш-им
Acc. same as nom. or gen.	на́ш-у	на́ше	same as nom. or gen.
Inst. наш-им	на́ш-ей(-ею)	на́ш-им	на́ш-ими
Prep. о на́ш-ем	о на́ш-ей	о на́ш-ем	о на́ш-их

NOTE

Ваш (your, *pl. or polite*) is declined in the same way.

ALL			
	SINGULAR		PLURAL
MASC.	FEM.	NEUTER	ALL GENDERS
Nom. весь	вся	всё	все
Gen. вс-его́	вс-ей	вс-его́	вс-ех
Dat. вс-ему́	вс-ей	вс-ему́	вс-ем
Acc. same as nom. or gen.	вс-ю	всё	same as nom. or gen.
Inst. вс-ем	вс-ей(-ею)	вс-ем	вс-е́ми
Prep. обо вс-ём	обо вс-ей	обо вс-ём	обо вс-ех

	SINGULAR			PLURAL
	THIS			THESE
	MASC.	FEM.	NEUTER	ALL GENDERS
Nom.	э́тот	э́та	э́то	э́ти
Gen.	э́т-ого	э́т-ой	э́т-ого	э́т-их
Dat.	э́т-ому	э́т-ой	э́т-ому	э́т-им
Acc.	same as nom. or gen.	э́т-у	э́то	same as nom. or gen.
Inst.	э́т-им	э́т-ой	э́т-им	э́т-ими
Prep.	об э́т-ом	об э́т-ой	об э́т-ом	об э́т-их

	SINGULAR			PLURAL
	THAT			THOSE
	MASC.	FEM.	NEUTER	ALL GENDERS
Nom.	тот	та	то	те
Gen.	т-ого́	т-ой	т-ого́	т-ех
Dat.	т-ому́	т-ой	т-ому́	т-ем
Acc.	same as nom. or gen.	т-у	т-о	same as nom. or gen.
Inst.	т-ем	т-ой	т-ем	т-е́ми
Prep.	о т-ом	о т-ой	о т-ом	о т-ех

	SINGULAR			PLURAL
	ONESELF			THEMSELVES
	MASC.	FEM.	NEUTER	ALL GENDERS
Nom.	сам	сама́	само́	са́ми
Gen.	сам-ого́	сам-о́й	сам-ого́	сам-и́х
Dat.	сам-ому́	сам-о́й	сам-ому́	сам-и́м
Acc.	same as nom. or gen.	сам-у́	сам-о́	same as nom. or gen.
Inst.	сам-и́м	сам-о́й	сам-и́м	сам-и́ми
Prep.	о сам-о́м	о сам-о́й	о сам-о́м	о сам-и́х

QUIZ 3

Fill in the blanks with the proper form of что.

1. Я не зна́ю, _____ э́то. I don't know what it is.
2. _____ но́вого? What's new?

3. _____ вы пи́шете? What are you writing?
4. Для _____ э́то? What's this for?
5. К _____ всё э́то? What's all this for?
6. _____ быть–того́ не минова́ть. What's to be, will be.
7. _____ вы удивля́етесь? What are you surprised at?
8. О _____ вы говори́те? What are you talking about?
9. В _____ де́ло? What's the matter?
10. _____ вы пи́шете? What are you writing with?

ANSWERS

1. что 2. Что 3. Что 4. чего́ 5. чему́ 6. Чему́ 7. Чему́ 8. чём
9. чём 10. Чем.

LESSON 11

A. NUMBERS 1–10

оди́н	one
два	two
три	three
четы́ре	four
пять	five
шесть	six
семь	seven
во́семь	eight
де́вять	nine
де́сять	ten

B. DAYS AND MONTHS[1]

понеде́льник	Monday
вто́рник	Tuesday
среда́	Wednesday

---

[1] Neither the names of the days nor of the months are capitalized unless they are found at the beginning of a sentence.

четве́рг	Thursday
пя́тница	Friday
суббо́та	Saturday
воскресе́нье	Sunday
янва́рь	January
февра́ль	February
март	March
апре́ль	April
май	May
ию́нь	June
ию́ль	July
а́вгуст	August
сентя́брь	September
октя́брь	October
ноя́брь	·November
дека́брь	December

C. Seasons and Directions

весна́	spring
весно́й	in the spring
ле́то	summer
ле́том	in the summer
о́сень	autumn
о́сенью	in the autumn
зима́	winter
зимо́й	in the winter
се́вер	north
юг	south
восто́к	east
за́пад	west

D. Word Study

ма́льчик	boy
де́вочка	girl

показывать-показать	to show
свобо́дный	free
повторя́ть-повтори́ть	to repeat
иногда́	sometimes
ме́дленно	slowly

LESSON 12

A. GREETINGS

у́тро	morning
у́тром	in the morning
день	day
днём	during the day (afternoon)
ве́чер	evening
ве́чером	in the evening
ночь	night
но́чью	during the night
сего́дня	today
вчера́	yesterday
за́втра	tomorrow
до́брое	good
у́тро	morning
До́брое у́тро.	Good morning.
до́брый	good
день	day/afternoon
До́брый день.	Good day. Good afternoon.
ве́чер	evening
До́брый ве́чер.	Good evening.
как	how
дела́	things
Как дела́?	How are things?
как	how

вы	you
себя́	yourself
чу́вствуете	feel
Как вы себя́ чу́вствуете?	How are you feeling?
спаси́бо	thank you
хорошо́	well
Спаси́бо, хорошо́.	Well, thank you.
ничего́	nothing
Спаси́бо, ничего́.	Thank you, not bad.
нельзя́	impossible [one may not]
лу́чше	better
Как нельзя́ лу́чше.	Couldn't be any better.
А вы?	And you?
То́же хорошо́, спаси́бо.	Also well, thank you.
Прекра́сно.	Excellent.
Что но́вого?	What's new?
Всё по-ста́рому.	Everything's the same [all as of old].

B. Last Month, Last Year, etc.

послеза́втра	day after tomorrow
че́рез два дня	in two days
че́рез пять дней	in five days
че́рез ме́сяц	in a month
на про́шлой неде́ле	last week
две неде́ли тому́ наза́д	two weeks ago
в про́шлом ме́сяце	last month
в про́шлом году́	last year
позавчера́	day before yesterday
вчера́ ве́чером	yesterday evening
за́втра у́тром	tomorrow morning

три дня тому́ наза́д   three days ago
ме́сяц тому́ наза́д   a month ago

QUIZ 4

Match the Russian terms with their English translations.

1.	среда́	a.	in the evening
2.	семь	b.	north
3.	март	c.	tomorrow
4.	сего́дня	d.	Thank you.
5.	Как дела́?	e.	Well, thank you.
6.	ве́чером	f.	Good evening.
7.	день	g.	Tuesday
8.	се́вер	h.	Wednesday
9.	вто́рник	i.	Monday
10.	октя́брь	j.	winter
11.	Спаси́бо.	k.	seven
12.	восто́к	l.	in the morning
13.	ле́то	m.	impossible [one may not]
14.	До́брый ве́чер.	n.	today
15.	нельзя́	o.	summer
16.	за́втра	p.	March
17.	у́тром	q.	east
18.	понеде́льник	r.	day
19.	зима́	s.	October
20.	Спаси́бо, хорошо́	t.	How are you?

ANSWERS

1—h; 2—k; 3—p; 4—n; 5—t; 6—a; 7—r; 8—b; 9—g; 10—s; 11—d; 12—q; 13—o; 14—f; 15—m; 16—c; 17—l; 18—i; 19—j; 20—e.

LESSON 13

A. COMMON VERB FORMS

Russian verbs have two conjugations. Infinitives of most verbs belonging to the first conjugation end with

-ать or -ять. Infinitives of verbs belonging to the second conjugation end with -еть or -ить. Although this is true of a great number of Russian verbs, there are many exceptions, which will be explained as they appear in the text.

Following are typical conjugations in the present tense:

FIRST CONJUGATION

ЧИТА́ТЬ	TO READ
я чита́ю	I read
ты чита́ешь	you read
он чита́ет	he reads
мы чита́ем	we read
вы чита́ете	you read
они́ чита́ют	they read

ЗНАТЬ	TO KNOW
я зна́ю	I know
ты зна́ешь	you know
он зна́ет	he knows
мы зна́ем	we know
вы зна́ете	you know
они́ зна́ют	they know

ПОНИМА́ТЬ	TO UNDERSTAND
я понима́ю	I understand
ты понима́ешь	you understand
он понима́ет	he understands
мы понима́ем	we understand
вы понима́ете	you understand
они́ понима́ют	they understand

ДУ́МАТЬ	TO THINK
я ду́маю	I think
ты ду́маешь	you think
он ду́мает	he thinks
мы ду́маем	we think
вы ду́маете	you think
они́ ду́мают	they think

ПИСА́ТЬ[1]	TO WRITE
я пишу́	I write
ты пи́шешь	you write
он пи́шет	he writes
мы пи́шем	we write
вы пи́шете	you write
они́ пи́шут	they write

Verbs ending with -нуть in the infinitive also belong to the first conjugation:

PERFECTIVE FUTURE

ВЕРНУ́ТЬ	TO RETURN, TO GIVE BACK
я верну́	I will return
ты вернёшь	you will return
он вернёт	he will return
мы вернём	we will return
вы вернёте	you will return
они́ верну́т	they will return

[1] C changes to ш, and the ending becomes у in the first-person singular and third-person plural.

SECOND CONJUGATION

ГОВОРИ́ТЬ	TO TALK, TO SPEAK
я говорю́	I talk
ты говори́шь	you talk
он говори́т	he talks
мы говори́м	we talk
вы говори́те	you talk
они́ говоря́т	they talk

ВИ́ДЕТЬ[1]	TO SEE
я ви́жу	I see
ты ви́дишь	you see
он ви́дит	he sees
мы ви́дим	we see
вы ви́дите	you see
они ви́дят	they see

ЗВОНИ́ТЬ	TO CALL, TO RING
я звоню́	I call
ты звони́шь	you call
он звони́т	he calls
мы звони́м	we call
вы звони́те	you call
они́ звоня́т	they call

[1] Д changes to ж in the first person.

MIXED CONJUGATION

хотéть	TO WANT
я хочý	I want
ты хóчешь	you want
он хóчет	he wants
мы хотúм	we want
вы хотúте	you want
онú хотя́т	they want

This verb in the singular has first-conjugation endings and changes the т to ч. In the plural it has second conjugation endings.

REFLEXIVE VERBS

Verbs ending in -сь or -ся are reflexive, with -ся usually coming after a consonant and -сь coming after a vowel. These verbs follow the general conjugation form, retaining the -ся ending after consonants and -сь after vowels:

занимáться	TO STUDY
я занимáюсь	I study
ты занимáешься	you study
он занимáется	he studies
мы занимáемся	we study
вы занимáетесь	you study
онú занимáются	they study

B. To Be or Not To Be: Быть

1. I AM

The verb *to be* is usually omitted in the present tense:

Я до́ма.	I am at home.
Мой дом о́чень удо́бный	My home is very comfortable.

2. I WAS AND I WILL BE

However, *to be* is used in the past and future tenses:

он был	he was
она́ была́	she was
оно́ бы́ло	it was
они́ бы́ли	they were

Я был до́ма.	I was at home.

Мой дом был удо́бный.	My home was comfortable.

я бу́ду	I will be
ты бу́дешь	you will be
он бу́дет	he will be
мы бу́дем	we will be
вы бу́дете	you will be
они́ бу́дут	they will be

Я бу́ду до́ма за́втра.	I will be home tomorrow.

Мой но́вый дом бу́дет о́чень удо́бный.	My new house will be very comfortable.

3. "To Be" as an Auxiliary

Быть (to be) is also used as an auxiliary verb in the imperfective future:

я бу́ду	I will
ты бу́дешь чита́ть	you will read
он бу́дет говори́ть	he will talk
мы бу́дем писа́ть	they will write
вы бу́дете etc.	you will etc.
они́ бу́дут	they will

C. The Past Tense

The past tense agrees with the gender of its subject. It is formed by dropping -ть from the infinitive and adding:

Masc.	-л	он чита́л	he was reading
Fem.	-ла	она́ говори́ла	she was speaking
Neut.	-ло	пальто́ висе́ло	the coat was hanging
Plur.	-ли	они́ звони́ли	they were calling

D. Word Study

и́мя	name
получа́ть-получи́ть	to receive
до́лго	for a long time
приве́т	greeting
за́втра	tomorrow
знамени́тый	famous
гро́мко	loudly
вре́мя	time
бога́тый	rich
коне́чно	of course

LESSON 14

A. HAVE AND HAVE NOT

Есть у вас маши́на?	Do you have a car?
У неё нет маши́ны.	She doesn't have a car.
У меня́ есть каранда́ш.	I have a pencil.
У меня́ нет карандаша́.	I don't have a pencil.
Есть у тебя́ газе́та?	Do you have a newspaper?
У тебя́ нет газе́ты.	You don't have a newspaper.
У него́ есть жена́ и сын.	He has a wife and a son.
У неё нет му́жа.	She doesn't have a husband.
У нас нет де́нег.	We don't have (any) money.
У вас есть ка́рта Москвы́?	Do you have a map of Moscow?
У вас нет ка́рты Москвы́.	You don't have a map of Moscow.
У них нет вре́мени.	They don't have time.
У меня́ есть вре́мя.	I have time.
У меня́ нет вре́мени.	I don't have time.
Вот хоро́ший магази́н; у них есть всё, что вам ну́жно.	Here's a good store; they have everything you need.
Вот мой друг.	Here is my friend.
У него́ нет друзе́й.	He has no friends.
У вас есть сигаре́ты?	Do you have cigarettes?

| **У меня́ нет спи́чек.** | I don't have (any) matches. |
| **У кого́ есть спи́чки?** | Who has matches? |

NOTE

1. In Russian, possession is usually expressed by the following form:

у меня́ есть	I have [by me is/are]
у тебя́ есть	you have [by you is/are *fam.*]
у него́ есть	he has [by him is/are]
у неё есть	she has [by her is/are]
у нас есть	we have [by us is/are]
у вас есть	you have [by you is/are *pl.* and *pol. sing.*]
у них есть	they have [by them is/are]

2. When the negative is used, the object of the negative is in the genitive case:

| **У меня́ нет карандаша́.** | I do not have a pencil. [By me is not a pencil.] |
| **У вас нет сестры́.** | You do not have a sister. [By you is not a sister.] |

3. If you want to know if someone has the thing you are looking for or the thing you need, use the word есть. However, if you want to know who has something you know is there, then omit the verb есть.

SUPPLEMENTAL VOCABULARY 2: FAMILY AND RELATIONSHIPS

mother	мать (f.), ма́тери (gen., sg.)
father	оте́ц, (m.), отца́ (gen., sg.)
son	сын (m.), сыновья́ (nom., pl.), сынове́й (gen., pl.)

daughter	дочь (f.), дочери (gen., sg.)
sister	сестра (f.), сёстры (nom., sg.), сестёр (gen., pl.)
baby	ребёнок (m.), дети (nom., pl.), младенец (m.), младенца (gen., sg.)
brother	брат (m.), братья (nom., pl.), братьев (gen., pl.)
husband	муж (m.), мужья (nom., pl.), мужей (gen., pl.)
wife	жена (f.), жёны (nom., pl.)
aunt	тётя (f.)
uncle	дядя (m.)
grandmother	бабушка (f.)
grandfather	дедушка (m.)
cousin	двоюродный брат (m.), двоюродная сестра (f.)
mother-in-law	тёща (f.) (мать жены), свекровь (f.) (мать мужа)
father-in-law	свёкор (m.) (отец жены), тесть (m.) (отец мужа)
stepmother	мачеха (f.), приёмная мать
stepfather	отчим (m.), приёмный отец
stepson	пасынок (m.), приёмный сын

stepdaughter	падчерица (f.), приёмная дочь
boyfriend	друг (m.), бойфренд (coll.)
girlfriend	подруга(f.), гёрлфренд (coll.)
fiancé(e)	невеста (f.), жених (m.)
friend	друг (m.), друзья (nom., pl.), друзей (gen., pl.)
relative	родственник (m.)
to love	любить – полюбить
to know (a person)	знать
to meet (a person)	встречать – встретить[1]
to marry (someone)	выходить – выйти замуж за (кого?), жениться (imper./perf.) на (ком?)
to divorce (someone)	разводиться – развестись с (кем?)
to get a divorce	получать – получить развод (m.)
to inherit	унаследовать (imper./perf.)

B. TO WANT AND TO FEEL LIKE

These are impersonal verb forms and adverb forms with the dative:

[1] When a verb is translated, both imperfective forms (in this order) are given. Bi-aspectual verbs, such as унаследовать (to inherit), are marked as "imper./perf." If either of the forms is not common, it is omitted.

1. "To want" is expressed by the verb хотéть.

2. "To feel like" is expressed by the reflexive verb хóчется with the dative case:

Он хóчет есть.	He is hungry. [He wants to eat.]
Я хочý пить.	I want a (to) drink.
Мне хóчется . . .	I feel like [to me it is wanting] . . .
Мне хóчется пить.	I'm thirsty. [I feel like drinking.]
Мы хотим читáть.	We want to read.
Они хотят спать.	They want to sleep.
Мне хóчется спать.	I feel like sleeping.
Емý хóчется есть.	He feels like eating.
Им хóчется пойти в кинó.	They feel like going to the movies.

3. The same form and construction are used with the following verbs:

нрáвиться	to please, to like
казáться	to seem
Мне нрáвится этот гóрод.	I like this city. [To me is pleasing this city.]
Мне кáжется, что я вас знáю.	It seems to me that I know you. [To me it seems, etc.]

4. The same form and construction are used with the following adverbs:

хóлодно	cold
жáрко	hot

тепло́	warm
прия́тно	pleasant
легко́	easy
интере́сно	interesting
стра́нно	strange

Мне хо́лодно.	I am cold. [To me it is cold.]
Ему́ жа́рко.	He is hot. [To him it is hot.]
Ей тепло́.	She is warm. [To her it is warm.]
Мне прия́тно.	It's nice/ pleasant. [To me it is pleasant.]
Нам легко́.	It is easy for us. [To us it is easy.]
Мне интере́сно.	I am interested. [To me it is interesting.]

C. PERSONAL PRONOUNS WITH PREPOSITIONS

All forms of personal pronouns beginning with vowels take the letter **н** when used with prepositions:

у него́ есть	he has
Мы зашли́ к нему́.	We went to see him.
Я рабо́тала с ни́ми.	I worked with them.

However, when **его́**, **её** and **их** are employed as modifiers, they do not take the **н** when used with prepositions:

| **у его́ бра́та есть** | his brother has |
| **Мы зашли́ в** | We went to their new |

их но́вый дом.   house.
Она́ пришла́ с её   She came with her
    сестро́й.   sister.

QUIZ 5

1. У него́ есть маши́на.	a. They have no time.
2. Ей здесь хо́лодно.	b. I feel like sleeping.
3. Вот моя́ кни́га.	c. He doesn't have a wife.
4. У них нет вре́мени.	d. This is their son.
5. Это их сын.	e. It's hot here.
6. Мне хо́чется спать.	f. She is cold here.
7. Тут жа́рко.	g. Who has matches?
8. Это о́чень далеко́.	h. Here is my book.
9. У него́ нет жены́.	i. He has a car.
10. У кого́ есть спи́чки?	j. It's very far.

ANSWERS

1—i; 2—f; 3—h; 4—a; 5—d; 6—b; 7—e; 8—j; 9—c; 10—g.

LESSON 15

A. Do You Speak Russian?

A general (yes/no) question in Russian is expressed
mostly by intonation, not by any particular construction of the sentence. "Do you speak Russian?" in
Russian is Вы говори́те по-ру́сски? [You speak by-
Russian?] The answer is: Говорю́ (Speak.) You do not
have to use the pronoun *I* (я), since the ending of the
verb говорю́ indicates the first person singular. Other
questions in Russian are formed with the help of question words (see Lessons 16 and 17).

Вы говори́те по-ру́сски?	Do you speak Russian?
Да, немно́го.	Yes, a little.
Не о́чень хорошо́.	Not very well.
Я говорю́ по-ру́сски.	I speak Russian.
Он говори́т по-англи́йски.	He speaks English.
Я говорю́ о́чень пло́хо.	I speak very badly.
Мы говори́м по-ру́сски о́чень ме́дленно.	We speak Russian very slowly.
Я зна́ю то́лько не́сколько слов.	I know only a few words.
Я могу́ сказа́ть то́лько не́сколько слов по-ру́сски.	I can say only a few words in Russian.
Ваш друг говори́т по-ру́сски?	Does your friend speak Russian?
Нет, не говори́т.	No, he doesn't.
Вы понима́ете по-ру́сски?	Do you understand Russian?
Да, понима́ю.	Yes, I understand (it).
Да, понима́ю, но не говорю́.	Yes, I understand but don't speak (it).
Я чита́ю, но не говорю́.	I read but do not speak (it).
Они́ понима́ют по-ру́сски о́чень хорошо́.	They understand Russian very well.
Вы пло́хо произно́сите ру́сские слова́.	You pronounce Russian words badly.
Э́то о́чень тру́дное сло́во.	That's a very difficult word.

Мне нужна́ пра́ктика.	I need practice.
Вы понима́ете меня́?	Do you understand me?
Да, я вас понима́ю.	Yes, I understand you.
Нет, я вас не понима́ю.	No, I don't understand you.
Что вы сказа́ли?	What did you say?
Вы говори́те сли́шком бы́стро.	You speak too fast.
Не говори́те так бы́стро.	Don't talk so fast.
Мне тру́дно понима́ть, когда́ вы говори́те так бы́стро.	It's difficult for me to understand when you speak so fast.
Говори́те ме́дленнее.	Speak more slowly.
Пожа́луйста, говори́те немно́го ме́дленнее.	Please speak a little more slowly.
Прости́те, но я не понима́ю вас.	Excuse me, but I don't understand you.
Пожа́луйста, повтори́те.	Please repeat.
Вы понима́ете меня́ тепе́рь?	Do you understand me now?
Да, тепе́рь я понима́ю.	Yes, now I understand.
Я хочу́ хорошо́ говори́ть по-ру́сски.	I want to speak Russian well.
Вы говори́те по-англи́йски?	Do you speak English?

B. THE WEATHER

Кака́я сего́дня пого́да?	What's the weather today?
Идёт дождь.	It's raining.
Идёт снег.	It's snowing.
Сейча́с хо́лодно.	It's cold.
Сейча́с па́смурно.	It's cloudy.
Сейча́с тепло́.	It's warm.
Сейча́с прия́тно.	It's nice.
Сейча́с жа́рко.	It's hot.
Сейча́с со́лнечно.	It's sunny.
Сейча́с ве́трено.	It's windy.
Како́й прогно́з на за́втра?	What's the forecast for tomorrow?

SUPPLEMENTAL VOCABULARY 3: WEATHER

It's raining.	Идёт дождь (m.).
It's snowing.	Идёт снег (m.).
It's hailing.	Идёт град (m.).
It's windy.	Дует ветер (m.)./ Ветрено.
It's hot.	Жарко.
It's cold.	Холодно.
It's sunny.	Светит солнце (n.)./ Солнечно.
It's cloudy.	Облачно.
It's beautiful.	Чудесно./Прекрасно.
storm	шторм (m.) (на море)
thunderstorm	гроза (f.)
wind	ветер (m.)
sun	солнце (n.)
thunder	гром (m.)
lightening	молния (f.)

hurricane	ураган (m.)
temperature	температура (f.)
degree	градус (m.)
rain	дождь (m.)
snow	снег (m.)
cloud	облако (n.)
fog	туман (m.)
smog	смог (m.)
umbrella	зонт (m.)

C. Word Study

вéжливый	polite
бéдный	poor
брать-взять	to take
дорогóй	expensive, dear
жизнь	life
вéчер	evening
весёлый	cheerful
скóлько	how much
опя́ть	again
мáло	little
наýка	science

QUIZ 6

Fill in the blanks with the appropriate Russian word.

1. Вы _____ по-рýсски? Do you speak Russian?
2. Я _____, но не _____. I understand, but don't
   speak.
3. _____ мéдленнее. Speak more slowly.
4. Что вы _____? What did you say?
5. Я _____ тóлько нéсколько слов. I know only a
   few words.
6. Онá _____ по-рýсски óчень _____. She reads
   Russian very well.

7. Сейча́с _____. It's cold.
8. Не говори́те так _____. Don't talk so fast.
9. _____, но я вас не понима́ю. Excuse me, but I don't
   understand you.
10. Кака́я сего́дня _____? What's the weather today?

ANSWERS

1. говори́те; 2. понима́ю, говорю́; 3. Говори́те; 4. сказа́ли;
5. зна́ю; 6. чита́ет, хорошо́; 7. хо́лодно; 8. бы́стро;
9. Прости́те; 10. пого́да.

LESSON 16

A. WHAT, WHICH, AND WHERE

Кото́рый сейча́с час?	What time is it now?
В кото́ром часу́?	At what time?
Вот кни́га, кото́рую я чита́л.	Here is the book that I was reading.
Де́ло, кото́рое он на́чал, идёт хорошо́.	The business that he started is going well.
Како́й э́то краси́вый язы́к!	What a pretty language this is!
Кака́я сего́дня пого́да?	What kind of weather is it today?
Каку́ю кни́гу вы чита́ете?	What book are you reading?
О како́й кни́ге вы говори́ли?	What book were you talking about?
Како́е сего́дня число́?	What is the date today?

Како́е вино́ вы хоти́те: кра́сное и́ли бе́лое?	Which wine do you want: red or white?
Како́й он у́мный!	How clever he is!
Да́йте мне каку́ю-нибудь кни́гу.	Give me any book.
Како́й вы стра́нный челове́к!	What a strange person you are!
Кака́я она́ краси́вая де́вушка!	What a pretty girl she is!
Куда́ вы идёте?	Where are you going?
Я иду́ на рабо́ту.	I'm going to work.
Где ва́ша рабо́та?	Where do you work?
Я рабо́таю на Театра́льной пло́щади.	I work on Theatre Square.
Что на столе́?	What's on the table (location)?
На столе́ кни́ги, бума́га и каранда́ш.	Books, paper, and a pencil are on the table.
Куда́ вы положи́ли мою́ кни́гу?	Where did you put my book?
На стол.	On the table (direction).
Куда́ вы идёте обе́дать по́сле рабо́ты?	Where are you going to have dinner (to dine) after work?
Я иду́ домо́й.	I'm going home.
Я бу́ду обе́дать до́ма.	I will have dinner at home.
Отку́да вы?	Where are you from?
Я из Петербу́рга.	I'm from St. Petersburg.
Да что вы!	You don't say!
Я то́же отту́да.	I'm also from there.
Како́е совпаде́ние! Удиви́тельно!	What a coincidence! Amazing!

B.   Which, What

котóрый, котóрая,
котóрое, котóрые   } which, what
какóй, какáя,
какóе, какúе

"Which" and "what" are declined like adjectives
and must agree in gender, number, and case with the
nouns they modify.

Какóй красúвый   What a pretty house!
дом!

Here дом is masculine, nominative, and singular;
so is какóй.

На какýю   Which picture are you
картúну вы   looking at?
смóтрите?

Картúну is feminine, accusative, and singular; so
is какýю.

О какúх кнúгах   Which books were you
вы говорúли?   talking about?

Кнúгах is feminine, plural, and prepositional; so is
какúх.

C.   Where with the Accusative
and Prepositional

"Where" in Russian is rendered by:
Кудá "where to," "whither" (direction) is always
used with the accusative case.

Где "where is" (location) is always used with the prepositional case.

Я иду́ в шко́лу.	I go to school.
идти́ в шко́лу	to go to (direction)
Я рабо́таю в шко́ле.	I work in (the) school.
рабо́тать в шко́ле	to work in (location)
Кни́гу положи́ли на стол.	They put the book on the table.
положи́ть на стол	to put on (direction)
Кни́га лежи́т на столе́.	The book is lying on the table.
лежа́ть на столе́	to lie on (location)

QUIZ 7

1. _____ э́то краси́вый язы́к! What a pretty language this is!
2. _____ вы идёте по́сле рабо́ты? Where are you going after work?
3. _____ вы рабо́таете? Where do you work?
4. _____ вы положи́ли мою́ кни́гу? Where did you put my book?
5. О _____ кни́ге вы говори́те? What book you are talking about?
6. Кни́га, _____ я чита́ю, о́чень хоро́шая. The book which I am reading is very good.
7. Я положи́л её _____. I put it on the table.
8. Да́йте мне _____ кни́гу. Give me any book.
9. _____ она́ у́мная! How clever she is!
10. _____ э́то краси́вое пальто́! What a beautiful coat this is!

ANSWERS

1. Како́й; 2. Куда́; 3. Где; 4. Куда́; 5. како́й; 6. кото́рую; 7. на стол; 8. каку́ю-нибудь; 9. Кака́я; 10. Како́е.

LESSON 17

A. WHOSE?

Чей э́то дом?	Whose house is that?
Чей э́то каранда́ш?	Whose pencil is that?
Чья э́то кни́га?	Whose book is that?
Чья газе́та там на столе́?	Whose newspaper is [there] on the table?
Чьё э́то пальто́?	Whose coat is that?
Чьи э́то де́ти?	Whose children are these?
Чьи де́ньги она́ тра́тит?	Whose money does she spend?

Чей, чья, чьё, чьи (whose) agree in gender, number, and case with nouns they modify:

Чья кни́га?	Whose book?

Кни́га is feminine and nominative; so is чья.

На чью кни́гу вы смо́трите?	Whose book are you looking at?

Кни́гу is feminine and accusative; so is чью.

Чьим карандашо́м вы пи́шете?	Whose pencil are you writing with?

Карандашо́м is masculine and instrumental; so is чьим.

	MASC.	FEM.	NEUT.	PLUR. ALL GEND.
Nom.	чей	чья	чьё	чьи
Gen.	чьего	чьей	чьего	чьих
Dat.	чьему	чьей	чьему	чьим
Acc.	Same as nom. or gen.	чью	чьё	Same as nom. or gen.
Inst.	чьим	чьей(ёю)	чьим	чьими
Prep.	о чьём	о чьей	о чьём	о чьих

B. WHAT, HOW

Как вас зову́т?	What is your name? [How are you called?]
Как ва́ше и́мя?	What is your name?
Как её зову́т?	What is her name?
Как дела́?	How are things?
Как по-ру́сски . . . ?	What is the Russian for . . . ?
Как э́то пи́шется?	How is that spelled?
Как называ́ется э́та кни́га?	What is the name of this book?
Как называ́ется э́тот го́род?	What is the name of this city?
Как пройти́ на Тверску́ю у́лицу?	How do you get to Tverskaya Street?
Как вы ду́маете, он хорошо́ говори́т по-ру́сски?	What do you think, does he speak Russian well?
Как хорошо́ он говори́т по-ру́сски!	How well he speaks Russian!
Как здесь жа́рко!	How hot it is here!
Как вам нра́вится Москва́?	How do you like Moscow?

Как вам не сты́дно так бы́стро забы́ть меня́!	Aren't you ashamed to have forgotten me so quickly?
Как я ра́да, что встре́тила вас!	How glad I am that I met you!
Вот как!	Is that so!
Как прия́тно гуля́ть в саду́!	How pleasant it is to stroll in the garden!
Как ни стара́йтесь– ничего́ не вы́йдет.	No matter how you try, nothing will come of it.
Как бы не так!	Nothing of the sort!
Бу́дьте как до́ма.	Make yourself at home.
с тех пор, как	since
как ви́дно	apparently [as it is seen]
Э́то как раз то, что мне ну́жно!	It's just the thing I need!

C. THE DEMONSTRATIVE PRONOUN Э́ТО

Note the difference between: э́то, meaning "this is," "that is," and э́тот, э́та, э́то, meaning "this."

Э́то каранда́ш.	This is a pencil.
Э́тот каранда́ш мой.	This pencil is mine.
Э́то кни́га.	This is a book.
Э́та кни́га не моя́.	This book is not mine.

D. WORD STUDY

| переводи́ть-перевести́ | to translate |
| симпати́чный | nice, cute (coll.) |

о́коло	near
фотогра́фия	photograph
коне́ц	end
изуча́ть-изучи́ть	to study in depth
тёплый	warm
ве́тер	wind
страна́	country
доро́га	road

QUIZ 8

1. Как называ́ется э́тот го́род?
2. Как вам не сты́дно так ско́ро забы́ть меня́?
3. Как дела́?
4. Бу́дьте как до́ма.
5. Как бы не так!
6. Чьи э́ти де́ти?
7. Чей э́то каранда́ш?
8. Как прия́тно гуля́ть в саду́!
9. Как вас зову́т?
10. Как э́то пи́шется?
11. Как здесь жа́рко!
12. Как дойти́ до у́лицы Тверско́й?
13. Чей э́то дом?
14. Вот как!
15. Как по-ру́сски . . . ?
16. Как называ́ется э́та кни́га?
17. Как я рад, что встре́тил вас!
18. Как вы ду́маете, он хорошо́ говори́т по-ру́сски?

a. How pleasant it is to stroll in the garden!
b. What is the Russian for . . . ?
c. Make yourself at home.
d. Whose children are these?
e. How hot it is here!
f. What is your name?
g. Whose house is this?
h. How do you get to Tverskaya Street?
i. Is that so!
j. What is the name of this city?
k. How are things?
l. Whose pencil is that?
m. What is the name of this book?
n. Aren't you ashamed to have forgotten me so soon?
o. How glad I am that I met you!

p. What do you think, does he speak Russian well?
q. How is that spelled?
r. Nothing of the sort!

ANSWERS

1—j; 2—n; 3—k; 4—c; 5—r; 6—d; 7—l; 8—a; 9—f; 10—q; 11—e; 12—h; 13—g; 14—i; 15—b; 16—m; 17—o; 18—p.

LESSON 18

A. MEETING A FRIEND

До́брое у́тро.	Good morning.
Здра́вствуйте.	Hello.
Вы говори́те по-ру́сски?	Do you speak Russian?
Да, я говорю́ по-ру́сски.	Yes, I speak Russian.
А я не говорю́ по-англи́йски.	And I don't speak English.
Вы с ю́га?	Are you from the south?
Да, я из Кры́ма.	Yes, I'm from the Crimea.
Как давно́ (ог ско́лько вре́мени) вы уже́ в Соединённых Шта́тах?	How long (how much time) have you been in the United States?
Два ме́сяца.	Two months.
Вы бы́стро вы́учите англи́йский язы́к.	You will learn English quickly.
Э́тот язы́к не о́чень тру́дный.	This language is not very difficult.
Он гора́здо трудне́е, чем вы ду́маете.	It's far more difficult than you think.
Возмо́жно, вы пра́вы. Наве́рно, нам гора́здо ле́гче вы́учить ру́сский язы́к, чем вам вы́учить англи́йский.	You may be right. It's probably much easier for us to learn Russian than for you to learn English.
Вы говори́те по-ру́сски о́чень хорошо́.	You speak Russian very well.
Я жил в Крыму́ не́сколько лет.	I lived in the Crimea for several years.

У вас прекра́сное произноше́ние.	Your pronunciation is excellent. [You have excellent pronuncia-tion.]
Спаси́бо, но всё же мне ну́жно бо́льше говори́ть (ог мне нужна́ пра́ктика).	Thank you, but all the same I need to speak more (I need practice).
Мне ну́жно идти́. Мой по́езд ско́ро отхо́дит.	I have to go. My train is leaving soon.
Всего́ хоро́шего и счастли́вого пути́.	All the best, and have a pleasant trip.
Жела́ю и вам того́ же. До свида́ния.	The same to you. Good-bye.
До свида́ния.	Good-bye.

QUIZ 9

Choose the correct word:

1. Она́ _____ (speaks) по-ру́сски.
   a. говорю́
   b. чита́ет
   c. говори́т

2. Я _____ (don't speak) по-англи́йски.
   a. чита́ю
   b. не говорю́
   c. говори́т

3. Я _____ (lived) в Крыму́.
   a. рабо́таю
   b. жить
   c. жил

4. Ру́сский _____ (easier) чем англи́йский.
   a. ле́гче
   b. бо́льше
   c. хорошо́

5. Кака́я _____ (today) пого́да?
   a. за́втра
   b. вчера́
   c. сего́дня

6. Как называ́ется э́тот _____ (city)?
   a. кни́га
   b. го́род
   c. у́лица

7. Я иду́ _____ (home).
   a. до́ма
   b. домо́й
   c. в до́ме

8. Куда́ вы _____ (are going)?
   a. иду́
   b. идёт
   c. идёте

9. _____ (What) сего́дня число́?
   a. Како́е
   b. Что
   c. Как

10. _____ (Which) тепе́рь час?
    a. Како́е
    b. Кото́рый
    c. Каку́ю

11. _____ (Where) вы рабо́таете?
    a. Где
    b. Куда́
    c. Как

12. _____ (Where) вы положи́ли кни́гу?
    a. Где
    b. Куда́
    c. Как

13. Вы говори́те сли́шком _____ (fast).
    a. пло́хо
    b. бы́стро
    c. ти́хо

14. Я _____ (you) не понима́ю.
   a. вам
   b. вы
   c. вас

15. _____ (he has) нет друзе́й.
   a. У него́
   b. У меня́
   c. У вас

16. _____ (She has) нет му́жа.
   a. У меня́
   b. У неё
   c. У него́

17. _____ (I am) хо́лодно.
   a. Мне
   b. Ему́
   c. Вам

18. _____ (She is) жа́рко.
   a. Мне
   b. Ей
   c. Её

19. Вот _____ (good) магази́н.
   a. хоро́ший
   b. до́брый
   c. плохо́й

20. Они́ _____ (want) спать.
   a. хочу́
   b. хо́чешь
   c. хотя́т

ANSWERS

1—c; 2—b; 3—c; 4—a; 5—c; 6—b; 7—b; 8—c; 9—a; 10—b;
11—a; 12—b; 13—b; 14—c; 15—a; 16—b; 17—a; 18—b; 19—a;
20—c.

B. Introductions

1. Pleased to Meet You

Разреши́те предста́виться.	Allow me to introduce myself.
Меня́ зову́т Ива́н.	My name is John.
Меня́ зову́т Мари́я.	My name is Mary.
О́чень прия́тно.	Pleased to meet you.
Я хоте́ла бы предста́вить вас И́горю.	I'd like to introduce you to Igor.
Отку́да вы?	Where are you from?
Я живу́ в США.	I live in the U.S.
Я живу́ в А́нглии.	I live in England.
Я в командиро́вке.	I'm here on a business trip.

2. Are You Here on Vacation?

До́брый день!	Hello!
Разреши́те предста́виться. Меня́ зову́т Джéйн Бра́ун.	Allow me to introduce myself. My name is Jane Brown.
О́чень прия́тно с ва́ми познако́миться.	Pleased to meet you.
Меня́ зову́т Ива́н Семёнов.	My name is Ivan Semyonov.
О́чень прия́тно.	Pleased to meet you.
Вы здесь в о́тпуске?	Are you here on vacation?
Да. Я бу́ду в Москве́ ещё четы́ре дня.	Yes. I'll be here in Moscow another four days.
Жела́ю вам прия́тно провести́ вре́мя!	Have a pleasant time!

C. Word Study

совреме́нный	contemporary
нача́ло	beginning
портре́т	portrait
пра́вильно	correctly
люби́ть	to love
везде́	everywhere
рад	glad (adj.)
тру́дный	difficult
мир	world, peace

LESSON 19

A. Cardinal Numerals

оди́н	one
два	two
три	three
четы́ре	four
пять	five
шесть	six
семь	seven
во́семь	eight
де́вять	nine
де́сять	ten
оди́ннадцать	eleven
двена́дцать	twelve
трина́дцать	thirteen
четы́рнадцать	fourteen
пятна́дцать	fifteen
шестна́дцать	sixteen
семна́дцать	seventeen

восемна́дцать	eighteen
девятна́дцать	nineteen
два́дцать	twenty
два́дцать оди́н	twenty-one
два́дцать два	twenty-two
два́дцать три	twenty-three
три́дцать	thirty
три́дцать оди́н	thirty-one
три́дцать два	thirty-two
три́дцать три	thirty-three
со́рок	forty
со́рок оди́н	forty-one
со́рок два	forty-two
со́рок три	forty-three
пятьдеся́т	fifty
пятьдеся́т оди́н	fifty-one
пятьдеся́т два	fifty-two
пятьдеся́т три	fifty-three
шестьдеся́т	sixty
шестьдеся́т оди́н	sixty-one
шестьдеся́т два	sixty-two
шестьдеся́т три	sixty-three
се́мьдесят	seventy
се́мьдесят оди́н	seventy-one
се́мьдесят два	seventy-two
се́мьдесят три	seventy-three
во́семьдесят	eighty
во́семьдесят оди́н	eighty-one
во́семьдесят два	eighty-two
во́семьдесят три	eighty-three
девяно́сто	ninety
девяно́сто оди́н	ninety-one
девяно́сто два	ninety-two
девяно́сто три	ninety-three
сто	one hundred

сто оди́н	one hundred one
сто два	one hundred two
сто три	one hundred three
сто два́дцать	one hundred twenty
сто три́дцать	one hundred thirty
сто три́дцать оди́н	one hundred thirty-one
сто три́дцать два	one hundred thirty-two
сто три́дцать три	one hundred thirty-three
две́сти	two hundred
три́ста	three hundred
четы́реста	four hundred
пятьсо́т	five hundred
шестьсо́т	six hundred
семьсо́т	seven hundred
восемьсо́т	eight hundred
девятьсо́т	nine hundred
ты́сяча	one thousand
миллио́н	one million
миллиа́рд	one billion

B. CASES WITH CARDINAL NUMERALS

оди́н (*m*), одна́ (*f.*), одно́ (*n.*), одни́ (*pl.*)
два (*m.*), две (*f.*), два (*n.*)

1. When the cardinal numeral is used in the nominative case:

The nominative singular is used after оди́н, одна́, одно́.
The nominative plural is used after одни́.
The genitive singular is used after два, две, три, четы́ре.
The genitive plural is used after пять, шесть, семь, etc.

2. When the number is compound, the case of the noun depends on the last digit:

Sing.	два́дцать оди́н каранда́ш	twenty-one pencils
Gen. *Sing.*	два́дцать два карандаша́	twenty-two pencils
Gen. *Pl.*	два́дцать пять карандаше́й	twenty-five pencils

C. DECLENSION OF NUMERALS

All cardinal numerals decline, agreeing with the noun they quantify, with the following exceptions:

a. When the noun is in the nominative case (as discussed above).

b. When the numeral is 2–4 in the accusative case (or a compound ending in 2–4) and the noun is inanimate, then the noun is in its genitive singular form.

c. When the numeral is 5–20 in the accusative case (or a compound ending in 5–20) then the noun is in its genitive plural form.

Gen. *Sing.*	**Я прочита́ла два письма́.**
	I read two letters.
Gen *Pl.*	**Он был там оди́н ме́сяц без двух дней.**
	He was there one month less two days.
Dat. *Pl.*	**Мы пришли́ к пяти́ часа́м.**
	We arrived by five o'clock.
Prep. *Pl.*	**Они́ говоря́т о семи́ кварти́рах.**
	They are speaking about seven apartments.

DECLENSION OF NUMERALS

	SINGULAR ONE			PLURAL ONLY (ALL GENDERS)
	MASC.	FEM.	NEUT.	
Nom.	оди́н	одна́	одно́	одни́
Gen.	одного́	одно́й	одного́	одни́х
Dat.	одному́	одно́й	одному́	одни́м
Acc.	Same as nom. or gen.	одну́	одно́	Same as nom. or gen.
Inst.	одни́м	одно́й(-о́ю)	одни́м	одни́ми
Prep.	об одно́м	об одно́й	об одно́м	об одни́х

	TWO	THREE	FOUR	FIVE
Nom.	два, две	три	четы́ре	пять
Gen.	двух	трёх	четырёх	пяти́
Dat.	двум	трём	четырём	пяти́
Acc.	Same as nom. or gen.	Same as nom. or gen.	Same as nom. or gen.	пять
Inst.	двумя́	тремя́	четырьмя́	пятью́
Prep.	о двух	о трёх	о четырёх	о пяти́

NOTE

All numbers from 6 to 20 follow the same declension pattern as 5.

QUIZ 10

1. Де́вять		a.	102
2. Два́дцать оди́н		b.	43
3. Двена́дцать		c.	600
4. Пятьдеся́т		d.	30
5. Пятна́дцать		e.	1,000
6. Со́рок три		f.	5
7. Четы́рнадцать		g.	9
8. Четы́реста		h.	15
9. Сто два		i.	50
10. Пять		j.	11
11. Шестьсо́т		k.	21
12. Ты́сяча		l.	80
13. Три́дцать		m.	400
14. Оди́ннадцать		n.	14
15. Во́семьдесят		o.	12

ANSWERS

1—g; 2—k; 3—o; 4—i; 5—h; 6—b; 7—n; 8—m; 9—a; 10—f;
11—c; 12—e; 13—d; 14—j; 15—l.

LESSON 20

A. ORDINAL NUMBERS

пе́рвый	first
второ́й	second
тре́тий	third
четвёртый	fourth
пя́тый	fifth
шесто́й	sixth

седьмо́й	seventh
восьмо́й	eighth
девя́тый	ninth
деся́тый	tenth
оди́ннадцатый	eleventh
двена́дцатый	twelfth
трина́дцатый	thirteenth
четы́рнадцатый	fourteenth
пятна́дцатый	fifteenth
шестна́дцатый	sixteenth
семна́дцатый	seventeenth
восемна́дцатый	eighteenth
девятна́дцатый	nineteenth
двадца́тый	twentieth
два́дцать пе́рвый	twenty-first
два́дцать второ́й	twenty-second
два́дцать тре́тий	twenty-third
тридца́тый	thirtieth
три́дцать пе́рвый	thirty-first
три́дцать второ́й	thirty-second
три́дцать тре́тий	thirty-third
сороково́й	fortieth
со́рок пе́рвый	forty-first
со́рок второ́й	forty-second
со́рок тре́тий	forty-third
пятидеся́тый	fiftieth
пятьдеся́т пе́рвый	fifty-first
пятьдеся́т второ́й	fifty-second
пятьдеся́т тре́тий	fifty-third
шестидеся́тый	sixtieth
шестьдеся́т пе́рвый	sixty-first
шестьдеся́т второ́й	sixty-second
шестьдеся́т тре́тий	sixty-third
семидеся́тый	seventieth
се́мьдесят пе́рвый	seventy-first
се́мьдесят второ́й	seventy-second

се́мьдесят тре́тий	seventy-third
восьмидеся́тый	eightieth
во́семьдесят пе́рвый	eighty-first
во́семьдесят второ́й	eighty-second
во́семьдесят тре́тий	eighty-third
девяно́стый	ninetieth
девяно́сто пе́рвый	ninety-first
девяно́сто второ́й	ninety-second
девяно́сто тре́тий	ninety-third
со́тый	hundredth
сто пе́рвый	hundred first
сто второ́й	hundred second
сто тре́тий	hundred third
сто двадца́тый	hundred twentieth
сто тридца́тый	hundred thirtieth
сто три́дцать пе́рвый	hundred thirty-first
сто три́дцать второ́й	hundred thirty-second
сто три́дцать тре́тий	hundred thirty-third
двухсо́тый	two hundredth
трёхсо́тый	three hundredth
четырёхсо́тый	four hundredth
пятисо́тый	five hundredth
шестисо́тый	six hundredth
семисо́тый	seven hundredth
восьмисо́тый	eight hundredth
девятисо́тый	nine hundredth
ты́сячный	thousandth
миллио́нный	millionth
миллиа́рдный	billionth

B. CHARACTERISTICS OF ORDINAL NUMERALS

All ordinal numerals are like adjectives, and decline as such:

MASC.	FEM.	NEUT.	PLUR.
пе́рвый	пе́рвая	пе́рвое	пе́рвые
второ́й	втора́я	второ́е	вторы́е

In compound forms, only the last digit changes, and only that digit is declined:

двадца́тый век   twentieth century

Это бы́ло три́дцать   That was on
   пе́рвого декабря́.   December 31.

тре́тий раз   third time

Втора́я мирова́я   The Second World War
   война́ ко́нчилась в   ended in 1945 [one
   ты́сяча девятьсо́т   thousand, nine hundred,
   со́рок пя́том году́.   forty-fifth year].

                  пя́тый год
                  пя́том году́   (prepositional singular)

C. WORD STUDY

река́	river
кли́мат	climate
рома́н	novel
находи́ться	to be located
висе́ть	to be hanging
расска́з	story
давно́	a long time ago
холо́дный	cold
чай	tea
господи́н	Mister

LESSON 21

A. Numbers in Context

Это двадца́тый уро́к.	This is the twentieth lesson.
Я уже́ зна́ю девятна́дцать уро́ков.	I already know nineteen lessons.
Я купи́ла но́вую шля́пу за ты́сячу рубле́й.	I bought a new hat for a thousand rubles.
Ско́лько вам лет?	How old are you?
Мне два́дцать лет.	I am twenty years old.
Ему́ два́дцать оди́н год.	He is twenty-one years old.
Ей три́дцать два го́да.	She is thirty-two years old.
Ива́ну Петро́вичу три́дцать пять лет.	Ivan Petrovich is thirty-five years old.
Я встаю́ в во́семь часо́в утра́.	I get up at eight o'clock in the morning.
Он рабо́тает с девяти́ утра́ до пяти́ часо́в ве́чера.	He works from nine in the morning until five [o'clock] in the evening.
Ско́лько сто́ит биле́т?	How much does a ticket cost?
(Биле́т сто́ит) сто пятьдеся́т рубле́й.	(A ticket costs) one hundred and fifty rubles.
Ско́лько сто́ит э́та руба́шка?	How much does this shirt cost?
(Э́та руба́шка сто́ит) ты́сячу пятьсо́т рубле́й.	This shirt costs one thousand five hundred rubles.

Это о́чень до́рого.	That's very expensive.
Это дёшево.	That's cheap.
Да́йте мне, пожа́луйста, другу́ю (f.).	Please give me another [a different one].
Покажи́те мне, пожа́луйста, э́ту кни́гу.	Please show me this book.
Каку́ю? Э́ту?	Which one? This one?
Нет, не э́ту, а ту, другу́ю.	No, not this, but that one.
Пожа́луйста.	Please.
Ско́лько она́ сто́ит?	How much does it cost?
Четы́реста три́дцать семь рубле́й.	Four hundred thirty-seven rubles.
Это не до́рого.	That's not expensive.
Я куплю́ её.	I'll buy it.
Когда́ я прие́хала в Москву́, я обменя́ла две́сти до́лларов.	When I arrived in Moscow, I exchanged two hundred dollars.
В э́той гости́нице де́вять этаже́й.	There are nine floors in this hotel.
Мой друг живёт на у́лице Пу́шкина, дом но́мер сто во́семьдесят четы́ре, кварти́ра два́дцать три.	My friend lives at 184 Pushkin Street, Apartment 23. [My friend lives on Pushkin street, house number one hundred eighty-four, apartment twenty-three.]
Его́ телефо́н 217-34-57.	His telephone number is 217-34-57.
Мой телефо́н 6-71-85.	My telephone number is 6-71-85.

B. How Old Are You?

"How old are you?" is expressed in Russian by the phrase Ско́лько вам (dative of вы) лет? [How many to you of years (of summers)?]

Мне два́дцать лет.   I am twenty years old.
[To me twenty years.]

After 20, use the genitive plural.

Мне со́рок пять лет.   I am forty-five years old.
[To me forty-five years.]

After 5, use the genitive plural.

Ему́ три́дцать оди́н   He is thirty-one years
год.   old. [To him thirty-one
years.]

After 1, use the nominative singular.

Ей два́дцать три   She is twenty-three years
го́да.   old. [To her twenty-
three years.]

After 3, use the genitive singular.

C. How Much, How Many

"How much?" and "how many?" are both expressed by one word in Russian: ско́лько.

Ско́лько э́то сто́ит?   How much does it cost?
Ско́лько раз я вам   How many times have I
э́то говори́ла?   told you that?

Ско́лько ученико́в в кла́ссе?	How many students are in the class?

After ско́лько and other adverbs of quantity— не́сколько (several), мно́го (many), ма́ло (little)— the genitive plural is usually used. If, however, the noun denotes an uncountable entity, such as вре́мя (time), вода́ (water) or вино́ (wine), the genitive singular is used.

QUIZ 11

1. Я купи́л но́вую шля́пу за _____ рубле́й. I bought a new hat for a thousand rubles.
2. Ей _____ го́да. She is thirty-two years old.
3. Я встаю́ в _____ часо́в утра́. I get up at eight o'clock in the morning.
4. У меня́ есть _____ до́лларов. I have two hundred dollars.
5. _____ сто́ит э́тот костю́м? How much does this suit cost?
6. _____ книг вы взя́ли домо́й? How many books did you take home?
7. Мой друг _____ на у́лице Пу́шкина. My friend lives on Pushkin Street.
8. Дом но́мер _____, кварти́ра _____. [House] Number 184, Apartment 23.
9. В э́той гости́нице _____ этаже́й. There are nine floors in this hotel.
10. Он рабо́тает с _____ утра́ до _____ ве́чера. He works from nine in the morning until five [o'clock] in the evening.

ANSWERS

1. со́рок ты́сяч; 2. три́дцать два; 3. во́семь; 4. две́сти; 5. Ско́лько; 6. Ско́лько; 7. живёт; 8. сто во́семьдесят четы́ре, два́дцать три; 9. де́вять; 10. девяти́, пяти́.

LESSON 22

A. I Like, I Don't Like

Мне о́чень нра́вится э́тот го́род.	I like this city very much.
Мне не нра́вится э́та у́лица.	I don't like this street.
Я люблю́ жить в дере́вне ле́том.	I love to live in the country during the summer.
В Нью-Йо́рке мно́го хоро́ших рестора́нов.	There are many good restaurants in New York.
Мне не нра́вится э́тот рестора́н.	I don't like this restaurant.
Како́й вку́сный ко́фе!	What delicious coffee!
Я всегда́ пью ко́фе с молоко́м.	I always drink coffee with milk.
Я не люблю́ молоко́.	I don't like milk.
Ко́фе без молока́ гора́здо вкусне́е.	Coffee without milk tastes much better [is much tastier].
Э́то де́ло вку́са.	It's a question of taste.
Како́е вку́сное пиро́жное!	What delicious pastry.
Переда́йте мне, пожа́луйста, са́хар-соль/ло́жку/нож/ви́лку/хлеб.	Please pass [me] the sugar/salt/spoon, knife/fork/bread.
Где моя́ салфе́тка?	Where is my napkin?

B. Telling Time

Telling time in Russian is rather complicated, but the simple form—два пятна́дцать (2:15), пять со́рок пять (5:45)—may always be used. Russians say:

2:05—пять мину́т тре́тьего (genitive of тре́тий)	five minutes of the third hour
2:55—без пяти́ три	without five: three
3:30—полови́на четвёртого (genitive of четвёртый)	half of the fourth
7:40—без двадцати́ во́семь	without twenty: eight
7:00 A.M.—семь часо́в утра́	seven o'clock in the morning
7:00 P.M.—семь часо́в ве́чера	seven o'clock in the evening
Ско́лько сейча́с вре́мени? (Кото́рый час?)	What time is it now? [Which is now the hour?]
Во ско́лько (в кото́ром часу́) отхо́дит по́езд?	When [at what hour] does the train leave?
Сейча́с двена́дцать часо́в дня, час дня.	It's now twelve noon, one o'clock in the afternoon.
Де́сять мину́т пя́того.	Ten minutes after four [ten minutes of the fifth (hour)].
Без че́тверти шесть.	A quarter [without a quarter] of six.
Де́сять часо́в утра́.	Ten o'clock in the morning.
Семь часо́в ве́чера.	Seven o'clock in the evening.
По́лдень.	Noon.
По́лночь.	Midnight.
Полови́на пе́рвого.	Half past twelve.
Полови́на второ́го.	Half past one.

Че́тверть тре́тьего.	A quarter after two [a quarter of the third].
Спекта́кль начина́ется без че́тверти во́семь.	The performance starts at a quarter of eight.
Э́та кни́га была́ напи́сана в ты́сяча девятьсо́т во́семь-десят пя́том году́.	This book was written in 1985 [one thousand, nine hundred, eighty-fifth year].

NOTE

After без (without), the genitive is used.

Мои́ часы́ отстаю́т.	My watch is slow.
Мои́ часы́ спеша́т.	My watch is fast.
Мои́ часы́ стоя́т.	My watch isn't running. [has stopped].

NOTE

Часы́ (watch or clock) is always used in the plural and takes a plural verb.

C. COMPARATIVE OF ADJECTIVES

To form the comparative of an adjective, drop the gender ending and add -ee for all gender endings and the plural. The adjective does not decline in the comparative:

краси́вый	pretty
краси́в-ее	prettier
тёплый	warm
тепл-е́е	warmer
весёлый	merry
весел-е́е	merrier

Irregular comparative forms:

хоро́ший	good
лу́чше	better
большо́й	big
бо́льше	bigger
ма́ленький	small
ме́ньше	smaller
широ́кий	wide
ши́ре	wider
у́зкий	narrow
у́же	narrower
плохо́й	bad
ху́же	worse
высо́кий	tall
вы́ше	taller
ти́хий	quiet
ти́ше	quieter
дорого́й	dear/expensive
доро́же	dearer/more expensive
просто́й	simple
про́ще	simpler
то́лстый	fat
то́лще	fatter

Москва́ бо́льше, чем Ха́рьков.	Moscow is larger than Kharkov.
Во́лга длинне́е Днепра́.	The Volga is longer than the Dnieper.
Нью-Йорк са́мый большо́й го́род в США.	New York is the largest city in the U.S.
Здесь (о́чень) хо́лодно.	It's (very) cold here.
Сего́дня холодне́е, чем вчера́.	It's colder today than yesterday.

Вчера́ бы́ло о́чень тепло́.	It was very warm yesterday.
Зимо́й на ю́ге тепле́е, чем на се́вере.	In the winter it's warmer in the south than in the north.
Рестора́н, где мы е́ли вчера́, вообще́, лу́чше.	The restaurant where we ate yesterday is better in general.
Пойдёмте туда́.	Let's go there.

D. SUPERLATIVE OF ADJECTIVES

The superlative of adjectives is formed in different ways. The simplest method, however, is to add са́мый, са́мая, са́мое, or са́мые (the most) to the adjective. For instance:

са́мый большо́й	the biggest
са́мая краси́вая	the prettiest
са́мые у́мные	the most clever

Са́мый declines with the adjective:

в са́мом большо́м до́ме	in the very largest house
Он пришёл с са́мой краси́вой же́нщиной.	He came with the prettiest woman.

QUIZ 12

1. Сего́дня холодне́е, чем вчера́.	a. The restaurant where we ate yesterday is better.
2. Я люблю́ жить в дере́вне ле́том.	b. Pass [me] the sugar, please.
	c. What time is it now?
3. Я бо́льше, чем мой брат.	d. Half-past twelve.

4. Какóй гóрод сáмый
   большóй в мирé?
5. Ресторáн, где мы éли
   вчерá, лýчше.
6. Онá всегдá пьёт кóфе
   с молокóм.
7. Передáйте мне,
   пожáлуйста, сáхар.
8. Кóфе без молокá
   горáздо вкуснéе.
9. Скóлько сейчáс
   врéмени?
10. Когдá (во скóлько)
    вы бýдете дóма?
11. Дéсять минýт пя́того.
12. Без десяти́ шесть.
13. Половина пéрвого.

14. Концéрт начинáется
    без чéтверти вóсемь.
15. Семь часóв вéчера.

e. The concert starts at a
   quarter to eight.
f. Coffee without milk
   tastes much better.
g. Ten minutes to six.

h. It's colder today than
   yesterday.
i. Which city is the largest
   in the world?
j. I love to live in the
   country in the summer.
k. She always drinks coffee
   with milk.
l. Ten minutes past four.
m. Seven P.M.
n. I am bigger than my
   brother.
o. When (at what time) will
   you be home?

ANSWERS

1—h; 2—j; 3—n; 4—i; 5—a; 6—k; 7—b; 8—f; 9—c; 10—o; 11—l;
12—g; 13—d; 14—e; 15—m.

LESSON 23

A. Negatives

Я ничегó не знáю.
Он ничегó не
  хóчет дéлать.
Не нáдо емý
  ничегó говори́ть.
Мне ничегó не нáдо.
Онá никудá не
  хóчет идти́.

I don't know anything.
He doesn't want to do
  anything.
You shouldn't tell
  him anything.
I don't need anything.
She doesn't want to go
  anywhere.

Они́ никогда́ не говоря́т, куда́ они́ иду́т.	They never say where they are going.
Тут о́чень темно́, я ничего́ не ви́жу.	It's very dark here; I can't see anything.
Никто́ не зна́ет, как дойти́ до библиоте́ки.	No one knows how to get to the library.
Я был в магази́не и ничего́ не купи́л.	I was at the store but didn't buy anything.
Я ещё нигде́ не́ был.	I haven't been anywhere yet.
Мы здесь уже́ две неде́ли и ещё не получи́ли ни одного́ письма́.	We have already been here two weeks and still haven't received one letter.

NOTE

A second (double) negative must be used with the following words:

ничего́	nothing
никто́	nobody
никогда́	never
никуда́	nowhere

Я ничего́ не зна́ю.	I don't know anything.
Никто́ не говори́т.	No one is speaking.
Мы никогда́ не́ бы́ли в Москве́.	We've never been to Moscow.

A negative adverb or pronoun must also use a negative with the verb it modifies. Negative words with не, on the other hand (не́чего, не́кого, не́когда, не́где, не́куда), are not used with a negated verb; they are used with infinitives and the semantic subject in the dative case.

Мне не́где жить.	There's nowhere for me to live.
Мне не́когда чита́ть.	I have no time to read.
Мне не́куда идти́.	I have nowhere to go.

B. PREDICATIVE FORM OF ADJECTIVES

Qualitative adjectives have two forms: the regular, which is called long, and a short form, so called because its ending is shortened. The masculine ends in a hard consonant, the feminine in -a, neuter in -o or -e, and plural in -ы or -и.

LONG	SHORT			
	MASC.	FEM.	NEUTER	PLURAL
ста́рый	стар	стара́	ста́ро	ста́ры

This short form is used only as a predicate and in literary language. Long forms are more common in Modern Russian.

Эта ста́рая кни́га лежи́т на столе́.	This old book is lying on the table.
Он стар. (outdated)	He is old (predicate).
Он старни́. (standard)	He is old.

C. ASKING DIRECTIONS

Я иностра́нец.	I'm a foreigner.
Я ничего́ не зна́ю в э́том го́роде.	I don't know anything about [in] this city.
Скажи́те, пожа́луйста, где здесь по́чта.	Please tell me where the post office is.

Два кварта́ла пря́мо, пото́м оди́н кварта́л напра́во.	Two blocks straight ahead, then one block to the right.
Большо́й дом на углу́, э́то по́чта.	The big building on the corner—that's the post office.
А что э́то за дом нале́во?	And what is this building on the left?
Э́то библиоте́ка.	That's the library.
Вы не зна́ете, где нахо́дится Большо́й теа́тр?	Do you know where the Bolshoi Theatre is?
Да, зна́ю.	Yes, I know.
Как туда́ прое́хать?	How do you get there?
Вам ну́жно сесть на тролле́йбус и прое́хать три остано́вки.	You have to take a trolleybus and go three stops.
Сойди́те на Театра́льной пло́щади, и там вы уви́дите Большо́й теа́тр.	Get off at Theatre Square, and there you'll see the Bolshoi Theatre.
А где остано́вка тролле́йбуса?	And where is the trolleybus stop?
На той стороне́ у́лицы. Вы мо́жете перейти́ на ту сто́рону то́лько на зелёный свет.	On that side of the street. You can cross to the other side only when the light is green.
Как ча́сто хо́дят тролле́йбусы?	How often do the trolleybuses run?
Ка́ждые пять мину́т.	Every five minutes.
Все тролле́йбусы на э́той остано́вке иду́т к Большо́му теа́тру?	Do all trolleybuses at that stop go to the Bolshoi Theatre?

Нет. То́лько тролле́йбус но́мер два. Но́мер двена́дцать идёт на вокза́л, а но́мер три́дцатьтри на пло́щадь Гага́рина.	No. Only trolleybus Number 2. Number 12 goes to the train station, and Number 13 goes to Gagarin Square.
Вы не зна́ете, что сего́дня идёт в Большо́м теа́тре?	And do [would] you know what is playing today at the Bolshoi Theatre?
Как же! Коне́чно зна́ю! Идёт «Лебеди́ное о́зеро».	What a question! Of course I do! *Swan Lake* is playing.
Что вы говори́те! Я давно́ хочу́ посмотре́ть э́тот бале́т.	You don't say! I've wanted to see that ballet for a long time.
Большо́е спаси́бо.	Thanks a lot.
О́чень вам благода́рен.	I'm very grateful to you.
Пожа́луйста.	You're welcome.

QUIZ 13

1. Он ничего́ не зна́ет.	a. I don't know where they were yesterday
2. Она́ ничего́ не хо́чет.	b. I don't know. I never know anything.
3. Мы никого́ не лю́бим.	c. She hasn't been anywhere yet.
4. Я не получи́л ни одного́ письма́.	d. I am a foreigner. I know nothing about [in] this town.
5. Что э́то за кни́га?	e. Thanks a lot.
6. Он давно́ хо́чет посмотре́ть э́тот бале́т.	f. Tell me, please, where the post office is.
7. Я иностра́нец. Я ничего́ не зна́ю в э́том го́роде.	g. I haven't received one letter.

8. Она́ ещё нигде́ не была́.	h. She doesn't want anything.
9. Скажи́те, пожа́луйста, где здесь по́чта?	i. What's playing at the theatre today?
10. Они́ никогда́ не говоря́т, куда́ они́ иду́т.	j. He has wanted to see this ballet for a long time.
11. Я не зна́ю, где они́ бы́ли вчера́.	k. We don't love anyone.
12. Что сего́дня идёт в теа́тре?	l. What sort of book is this?
13. Я не зна́ю. Я никогда́ ничего́ не зна́ю.	m. He doesn't know anything.
14. Большо́е спаси́бо.	n. You have to go three stops.
15. Вам ну́жно прое́хать три остано́вки.	o. They never say where they are going.

ANSWERS

1—m; 2—h; 3—k; 4—g; 5—l; 6—j; 7—d; 8—c; 9—f; 10—o;
11—a; 12—i; 13—b; 14—e; 15—n.

SUPPLEMENTAL VOCABULARY 4:
AROUND TOWN

town	го́род (m.), города́ (nom., pl.)
city	го́род (m.), города́ (nom., pl.)
village	дере́вня (f.)
car	маши́на (f.)
bus	авто́бус (m.)
train	по́езд (m.), поезда́ (nom., pl.)
taxi	такси́ (n.)
subway/metro	метро́ (n.)
traffic	движе́ние (n.)
building	зда́ние (n.)
apartment building	жило́е зда́ние (n.)
library	библиоте́ка (f.)

restaurant	ресторан (m.)
store	магазин (m.)
street	улица (f.)
park	парк (m.)
train station	вокзал (m.)/ станция (f.)
airport	аэропорт (m.)
airplane	самолет (m.)
intersection	перекрёсток (m.)
lamp post	фонарный столб (m.), фонарь (m.)
street light	светофор (m.)
bank	банк (m.)
church	церковь (f.), церкви (nom., pl.), церквей (gen., pl.)
temple	храм (m.)
mosque	мечеть (f.)
sidewalk	тротуар (m.)
bakery	булочная (f.) (shop) пекарня (f.) (facility)
butcher shop	мясной магазин (m.)
café/coffee shop	кафе (n.), кофейня (f.)
drugstore/pharmacy	аптека (f.)
supermarket	универсам (m.)
market	рынок (m.), на рынке
shoe store	обувной магазин (m.)
clothing store	магазин одежды
electronics store	магазин бытовой техники
bookstore	книжный магазин
department store	универмаг (m.)
mayor	мэр (m.)

city hall/municipal building	мэрия (f.), городской совет (m.)
to buy	покупать - купить
to go shopping	ходить - сходить за покупками
near/far	близко/далеко
urban	городской
suburban	пригородный
rural	сельский

LESSON 24

A. SAMPLE SENTENCES: SMALL TALK

Вчера́ бы́ло воскресе́нье.	Yesterday was Sunday.
Вчера́ никто́ не рабо́тал.	Yesterday no one was working.
Мы сиде́ли до́ма весь день.	We stayed home all day.
Ле́том на да́че бы́ло о́чень жа́рко.	It was very hot in the country during the summer.
Я был на ле́кции.	I was at the lecture.
Ле́ктор говори́л об Аме́рике.	The lecturer was talking about America.
Он сказа́л, что в Ю́жной Аме́рике говоря́т по-испа́нски и по-португа́льски.	He said that in South America they speak Spanish and Portuguese.
Я учи́л англи́йский язы́к, когда́ я был ещё ма́леньким ма́льчиком.	I studied English when I was still a small boy.

Толсто́й написа́л рома́н «Война́ и мир».	Tolstoi wrote the novel *War and Peace*.
Его́ жена́ ему́ всегда́ помога́ла.	His wife was always helping him.
Он мог рабо́тать по це́лым дням.	He could work for days at a time.
Она́ могла́ писа́ть мно́го часо́в в день.	She could write many hours a day.
Говоря́т, что она́ перепи́сывала э́тот рома́н де́сять раз.	They say that she copied this novel ten times.
Я уста́л.	I am tired.
Я устаю́, когда́ (я) мно́го говорю́.	I become tired when I talk a lot.
Он устава́л о́чень бы́стро.	He used to become tired very quickly.
Она́ опозда́ла.	She was late.
Она́ всегда́ опа́здывает.	She is always late.
Они́ шли домо́й, когда́ неожи́данно пошёл дождь.	They were walking home when it started to rain unexpectedly.
Дождь шёл це́лый день (весь день), всю неде́лю, весь ме́сяц.	It rained [rain fell] all day, all week, all month.
Секрета́рша пришла́ на рабо́ту и начала́ печа́тать.	The secretary arrived at work and began to type.
Он игра́л. Она́ слу́шала. Он ко́нчил игра́ть.	He played. She listened. He finished playing.
Она́ заговори́ла.	She began to speak.

В час дня все пошли обедать.	At one o'clock everyone went to have lunch.
Я пообедала и вернулась на работу.	I had lunch [lunched] and returned to work.
Он был здесь несколько дней тому назад.	He was here several days ago.
Я приехала в Москву две недели тому назад.	I came to Moscow two weeks ago.
Я ещё не получила ни одного письма.	I still haven't received a single letter.
Почта приходит рано утром.	The mail comes early in the morning.
Она думала, что здесь все говорят по-английски.	She thought that everyone spoke English here.
Она купила всё, что ей было нужно.	She bought everything [all] that she needed.
Он купил много ненужных вещей.	He bought a lot of unnecessary things.
Она любила его когда-то.	She loved him at one time.
И он любил её, но это было много лет тому назад.	And he loved her too, but that was many years ago.

B. Verbs: Perfective and Imperfective Aspects

Russian verbs can be perfective or imperfective. Imperfective verbs express continuous or repeated action. They have three tenses: past, present, and future.

Perfective verbs indicate completion of action, beginning of action, or both, and have only two tenses: past and future.

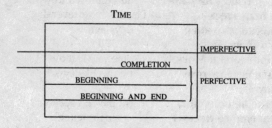

Some perfective verbs are formed by adding prefixes—such as с, на, вы, в, по—to imperfective verbs. When a prefix is added to a verb, very often the meaning of the verb is changed at the same time.

IMPERFECTIVE	PERFECTIVE
писа́ть to write	написа́ть to write down
	to finish writing
	переписать to copy

When the meaning of the verb changes, the new verb (переписа́ть, to copy) that has been formed must have its own imperfective. To form the imperfective of such new verbs, the suffix -ыв, -ив or -ав is added:

IMPERFECTIVE	PERFECTIVE	IMPERFECTIVE
писа́ть (to write)	переписа́ть (to copy)	перепи́сывать
чита́ть (to read)	прочита́ть (to finish reading or to read through)	прочи́тывать
	перечита́ть (to read over)	перечи́тывать
знать (to know)	узна́ть (to find out or to recognize)	узнава́ть

The past tense of the perfective is formed in the same manner as the past tense of the imperfective.

C. THE FUTURE TENSE

The future tense has two forms: imperfective future and perfective future. As has already been pointed out, the imperfective future is formed by using the auxiliary verb быть with the infinitive of the imperfective verb.

я бу́ду	I will
ты бу́дешь	you will
он бу́дет говори́ть, чита́ть	he will speak, read,
мы бу́дем понима́ть, etc.	we will understand, etc.
вы бу́дете	you will
они́ бу́дут	they will

The perfective future is formed without using the auxiliary verb быть.

PRESENT		PERFECTIVE FUTURE	
я пишу́	I write	я напишу́	I will write
ты говори́шь	you speak	ты ска́жешь	you will say
он идёт	he goes	он придёт	he will come
мы чита́ем	we read	мы прочита́ем	we will read
вы смо́трите	you look	вы посмо́трите	you will look
они́ е́дут	they go [ride]	они́ прие́дут	they will come [ride]

NOTE

The perfective verb is conjugated in the future in the same way that the imperfective is conjugated in the present.

QUIZ 14

1. Ле́ктор говори́л об
   Аме́рике.

2. Вчера́ я писа́л весь
   день.

3. Она́ написа́ла вчера́
   два письма́.

4. Он сказа́л, что он
   ничего́ не зна́ет.

5. Она́ всегда́ э́то
   говори́т.

6. Она́ опозда́ла
   сего́дня.

7. Дождь шёл це́лый
   день.

8. Она́ всегда́ опа́зды-
   вает.

9. В час дня все пошли́
   обе́дать.

10. Он купи́л мно́го
    нену́жных веще́й.

11. Я поза́втракал и
    верну́лся на рабо́ту.

12. Она́ была́ до́ма.

13. Он был в го́роде.

14. Мы бы́ли на
    рабо́те.

15. Он был в Аме́рике
    мно́го лет тому́ наза́д.

a. He was in town.

b. I had breakfast and returned
   to work.

c. She always says that.

d. At one o'clock everyone
   went to lunch.

e. She was home.

f. She is always late.

g. Yesterday I wrote all day.

h. She was late today.

i. He was in America many
   years ago.

j. He said that he knows
   nothing.

k. We were at work.

l. The lecturer was talking
   about America.

m. She wrote two letters yesterday.

n. It was raining all day.

o. He bought a lot of unneces-
   sary things.

ANSWERS

1—l; 2—g; 3—m; 4—j; 5—c; 6—h; 7—n; 8—f; 9—d; 10—o;
11—b; 12—e; 13—a; 14—k; 15—i.

LESSON 25

A. MEETING A FRIEND IN MOSCOW

Здра́вствуйте, Никола́й Ива́нович!	Hello, Nikolai Ivanovich.
Здравствуйте, Наде́жда Петро́вна, как давно́ я вас не ви́дел!	Hello, Nadezhda Petrovna, I haven't seen you in a long time.
Вы давно́ в Москве́?	Have you been in Moscow long?
Нет. Я прие́хал неде́лю тому́ наза́д.	No. I arrived a week ago.
Где вы живёте?	Where are you staying [living]?
Я живу́ у бра́та. У него́ больша́я кварти́ра.	I'm staying [living] with my brother. He has a large apartment.
Ваш брат хорошо́ говори́т по-англи́йски, пра́вда?	Your brother speaks English well, doesn't he? [isn't it true?]
Да. Он говори́т, пи́шет и чита́ет по-англи́йски.	Yes. He speaks, writes, and reads English.
Его́ жена́ америка́нка, да?	His wife is an American, isn't she?
Да, вот почему́ он так хорошо́ зна́ет англи́йский язы́к.	Yes, that's why he knows English so well.
Скажи́те, а как его́ жена́ говори́т по-ру́сски?	Tell me, how well does his wife speak Russian?
Не о́чень хорошо́.	Not very well.

Она́ понима́ет почти́ всё, но говори́т пло́хо.	She understands almost everything, but speaks poorly.
Вы давно́ зна́ете его́ жену́?	Have you known his wife for a long time?
Коне́чно. Я знал её ра́ньше моего́ бра́та.	Of course. I knew her before my brother did.
Говоря́т, что она́ о́чень ми́лая же́нщина.	They say that she's a very pleasant woman.
Да, она́ у́мная, краси́вая и о́чень ми́лая.	Yes, she's intelligent, pretty, and very pleasant.
У них есть де́ти?	Do they have children?
Да, есть.	Yes, they do.
А как они́ говоря́т– по-ру́сски и́ли по-англи́йски?	What do they speak— Russian or English?
Де́ти говоря́т и по-ру́сски и по-англи́йски.	The children speak both Russian and English.
Как э́то хорошо́! Я ду́маю, что все де́ти должны́ знать хотя́ бы два языка́.	Isn't that good! I think that all children should know at least two languages.
Ну, коне́чно, все должны́ знать два языка́.	Well, of course everybody should know two languages.
Вот вы–ру́сский и о́чень хорошо́ говори́те. по-англи́йски.	Well, you're Russian, and you speak English very well.
А вы–америка́нка и о́чень хорошо́ говори́те по-ру́сски.	And you're an American and speak Russian very well.

Нет, ещё не о́чень хорошо́, но я всё вре́мя занима́юсь и бу́ду хорошо́ говори́ть по-ру́сски.	No, not very well yet, but I'm studying all the time and will speak Russian well.
С кем вы занима́етесь?	With whom are you studying?
Ра́ньше у меня́ был о́чень хоро́ший учи́тель, но он уе́хал, потому́ что его́ мать заболе́ла. И тепе́рь я занима́юсь сама́.	I had a very good teacher before, but he went away because his mother became ill. And now I'm studying by myself.
Но вы зна́ете, э́то о́чень тру́дно.	But you know, that's very difficult.
Коне́чно, тру́дно занима́ться само́й, но я уже́ доста́точно мно́го прошла́, а чем бо́льше вы зна́ете, тем ле́гче продолжа́ть.	Of course it's difficult to study by oneself, but I've already gone through quite a lot, and the more you know, the easier it is to continue.

SUPPLEMENTAL VOCABULARY 5: AT SCHOOL

school	шко́ла (f.)
university	университе́т (m.)
classroom	класс (m.), аудито́рия (f.)
course	курс (m.)
teacher	учи́тель (m.), учителя́ (nom., pl.)
professor	профе́ссор (m.), профессора́ (nom., pl.)

student	студент (m.)
subject	предмет (m.)
notebook	тетрадь (f.)
textbook	учебник (m.)
math	математика (f.)
history	история (f.)
chemistry	химия (f.)
biology	биология (f.)
literature	литература (f.)
language	язык (m.)
art	искусство (n.)
music	музыка (f.)
gym	спортивный зал (m.)
recess	перемена (f.)
test	письменный экзамен (m.)
grade	класс (m.)
report card	дневник (m.)
diploma	диплом (m.)
degree	учёная степень (f.)
difficult/easy	сложно/легко
to study	учиться (imperf.)
to learn	изучать – изучить
to pass	сдавать – сдать
to fail	проваливать – провалить (что?), проваливаться – провалиться на
	• экзамене

B. THE PERSONAL PRONOUNS: Сам, Себя́

The personal pronoun сам, сама́, само́, са́ми (by oneself) is declined like other personal pronouns (see table, Lesson 11). It can modify the subject of the sentence, emphasizing that the action is performed independently, or a complement, with the meaning that it is a specific complement and not any other.

The reflexive pronoun себя (oneself) has no gender and no nominative form. It refers back to the subject.

Я занимаюсь сам.	I study by myself.
Я сказал ему самому.	I told him [himself].
Само собой. разумеется.	It goes without saying. [It reasons itself.]
Он разговаривает сам с собой.	He talks to himself. [himself with himself].
Он никогда сам о себе ничего не говорит.	He never says anything about himself.
Она взяла с собой мою книгу.	She took my book with her.
Она сама сшила себе платье.	She made a dress for herself.

The verb жить (to live), although it ends in -ить, belongs to the first conjunction and is conjugated as follows:

я живу	I live
ты живёшь	you live
он живёт	he lives
мы живём	we live
вы живёте	you live
они живут	they live

C. Word Study

строить-построить	to build
внимательно	attentively
кончать-кончить	to finish
памятник	monument

научный	scholarly
обсуждáть-обсудúть	to discuss
мéсяц	month
всегдá	always
покá	so long

QUIZ 15

1. Онá рýсская и óчень хорошó говорúт по-англúйски.
2. Где вы живёте?
3. Скажúте, как его женá говорúт по-рýсски?
4. У них есть дéти.

5. Вы давнó знáете егó?
6. Рáньше у меня был óчень хорóший учúтель.
7. Я всё врéмя занимáюсь.

8. Мы бýдем хорошó говорúть по-русски.
9. Онú приéхали в Москвý недéлю тому назáд.
10. Я занимáюсь сам.
11. Чем бóльше вы знáете, тем лéгче продолжáть.
12. Он уéхал, потомý что егó мать заболéла.
13. Все должны́ знать хотя́ бы два языкá.
14. С кем вы занимáетесь?

15. Я давнó вас не вúдел.

a. I study all the time.

b. They have children.
c. The more you know, the easier it is to continue.
d. I haven't seen you in a long time.
e. We will speak Russian well.
f. With whom are you studying?
g. She is Russian and speaks English very well.
h. He went away because his mother became ill.
i. Where do you live?

j. Have you known him long?
k. Tell me, how well does his wife speak Russian?
l. I had a very good teacher before.
m. They arrived in Moscow a week ago.
n. Everyone should know at least two languages.
o. I study by myself.

ANSWERS

1—g; 2—i; 3—k; 4—b; 5—j; 6—l; 7—a; 8—e; 9—m; 10—o; 11—c; 12—h; 13—n; 14—f; 15—d.

LESSON 26

A. SHOPPING: IN A STORE

Где здесь хоро́ший магази́н?	Where is there a good store here?
Како́й магазин вам ну́жен?	What kind of a store do you need?
Мне ну́жно купи́ть бума́гу, карандаши́ и словари́.	I have to buy paper, pencils, and dictionaries.
Есть тако́й магази́н на Не́вском проспе́кте.	There's a store like that on Nevsky Prospect.
(В магази́не)	(In the store)
У вас есть словари́?	Do you have dictionaries?
Коне́чно. Како́й слова́рь вам ну́жен?	Of course. What kind of dictionary do you need?
Я америка́нец, и как вы слы́шите, не совсе́м хорошо́ говорю́ по-ру́сски.	I'm an American, and, as you (can) hear, I don't speak Russian too well.
Очеви́дно, вам нужны́ ру́сско-англи́йский и а́нгло-ру́сский словари́. Вот о́ба словаря́ в одно́м то́ме, а вот побо́льше, в двух тома́х.	Obviously you need Russian-English and English-Russian dictionaries. Here are both dictionaries in one volume, and this one a bit larger, in two volumes.
Ско́лько они́ сто́ят?	How much do they cost?
Однотомный триста во́семьдесят рубле́й, а	The one-volume [dictionary] three hundred eighty rubles,

двухто́мный шестьсо́т.	and the two-volume, six hundred.
Как вы ду́маете, како́й из них лу́чше? Я не зна́ю.	What do you think— which of them is better? I don't know.
Это де́ло вку́са.	It's a question of taste.
Е́сли вы мно́го чита́ете и перево́дите, возьми́те большо́й.	If you read a lot and translate, take the big one.
Нет, мне ну́жен слова́рь то́лько для разгово́ра.	No, I need a dictionary only for conversation.
Ну, тогда́ возьми́те ма́ленький. Его́ удо́бно носи́ть с собо́й.	Well, then, take the lit- tle one. It's convenient to carry with you.
Скажи́те, пожа́луйста, а у вас есть карандаши́?	Tell me, please, do you have pencils?
Вот чёрные карандаши́, вот кра́сные и си́ние.	Here are black pencils; here are red and blue ones.
Э́ти твёрдые, а э́ти мя́гкие.	These are hard, and these are soft.
Покажи́те мне, пожа́луйста, перьевы́ру́чки.	Please show me (some) fountain pens.
Вот э́то о́чень хоро́шая ру́чка. Мы гаранти́руем, что она́ не бу́дет течь.	Here's a very good pen. We guarantee that it won't leak.
Ну, вот и хорошо́. Э́то, пожа́луй, всё.	That's good. I think that's all.
Да́йте мне двена́дцать карандаше́й,	Give me a dozen pencils, one pen,

одну́ ру́чку и вот э́ту коро́бку пи́счей бума́ги.	and that box of writing paper there.
А слова́рь вы не возьмёте?	Aren't you going to take the dictionary?
Ах да! Коне́чно! Да́йте мне ма́ленький, однотóмный.	Oh yes! Of course! Give me the little one-volume (dictionary).
Ско́лько с меня́?	How much do I owe you?
Слова́рь три́ста во́семьдесят рубле́й, карандаши́ три́дцать рубле́й, ру́чка сто де́сять рубле́й и бума́га се́мьдесят рубле́й—всего́ пятьсо́т девяно́сто рубле́й.	The dictionary is three hundred and eighty rubles; the pencils, thirty rubles; the pen, one hundred and ten rubles; and the paper, seventy rubles—in all, five hundred and ninety rubles.
Пожа́луйста.	Here you are.
Спаси́бо. Всего́ хоро́шего.	Thank you. All the best.
До свида́ния.	Good-bye.
Заходи́те ещё.	Come again!

B. PERFECTIVE VERBS WITH DIFFERENT ROOTS

IMPERFECTIVE	PERFECTIVE	IMPERFECTIVE
говори́ть (to speak)	сказа́ть (to tell)	
	заговори́ть (to begin talking)	заговáривать
	рассказа́ть (to tell a story)	расскáзывать

заказа́ть	зака́зывать
(to order something to be made or done)	
приказа́ть	прика́зывать
(to order, to command)	

Prefixes can be added to either говори́ть or каза́ть, but each combination forms a new verb; e.g.:

за-говори́ть	to begin talking
за-каза́ть	to order something
от-говори́ть	to talk someone out of something
от-каза́ть	to refuse

The perfective of the verb брать (*to take*) is взять. They are conjugated as follows:

PRESENT TENSE		PERFECTIVE FUTURE	
брать		взять	
я беру́	I take	я возьму́	I will take
ты берёшь	you take	ты возьмёшь	you will take
он берёт	he takes	он возьмёт	he will take
мы берём	we take	мы возьмём	we will take
вы берёте	you take	вы возьмёте	you will take
они беру́т	they take	они возьму́т	they will take

QUIZ 16

1. Вот о́ба словаря́ в одно́м то́ме.

2. Как вы ду́маете, како́й из них лу́чше?

3. Покажи́те мне, пожа́луйста, перьевы́е еру́чки.

4. Да́йте мне двена́дцать карандаше́й.

5. Как вы слы́шите, я не совсе́м хорошо́ говорю́ по-ру́сски.

a. These pencils are hard, and these are soft.

b. I need a dictionary only for conversation.

c. In all, one hundred seventy-six thousand rubles.

d. I came especially for that.

e. If you read and translate a lot, take the big one.

6. Мне ну́жен слова́рь то́лько для разгово́ра.

7. Я специа́льно за э́тим пришёл.

8. Ско́лько они́ сто́ят?

9. Всего́ сто се́мьдесят шесть ты́сяч рубле́й.

10. Очеви́дно, вам ну́жен большо́й хоро́ший слова́рь.

11. Е́сли вы мно́го чита́ете и перево́дите, возьми́те большо́й.

12. Э́ти карандаши́ твёрдые, а э́ти мя́гкие.

13. Мне ну́жен кни́жный магази́н.

14. Како́й слова́рь вам ну́жен?

15. Всего́ хоро́шего. Заходи́те ещё.

f. I need a bookstore.

g. Here are both dictionaries in one volume.

h. Give me twelve pencils.

i. Please show me (some) fountain pens.

j. What do you think—which of them is better?

k. How much do they cost?

l. All the best. Come again.

m. What kind of a dictionary do you need?

n. As you (can) hear, I don't speak Russian well.

o. Obviously you need a good, big dictionary.

ANSWERS

1—g; 2—j; 3—i; 4—h; 5—n; 6—b; 7—d; 8—k; 9—c; 10—o; 11—e; 12—a; 13—f; 14—m; 15—l.

LESSON 27

A. VERBS OF MOTION

Verbs of motion have many variations of meaning. A different verb is used to express movement by a conveyance than is used to express movement by foot.

Each of these verbs has two forms: i.e., one describes a single action in one direction; the other, a repeated action. All of these forms are imperfective. The perfective is formed by adding a prefix to a single-action verb. However, it must be emphasized that the addition of the prefix changes the meaning of the verb. The same prefix with the repeated-action verb forms the imperfective of the new verb.

Study the following chart.

IMPERFECTIVE	REPEATED ACTION		ONE ACTION	PERFECTIVE
	ходи́ть	to go on foot	идти́	
	е́здить	to go by vehicle	е́хать	
выходи́ть		to go out on foot		вы́йти
выезжа́ть		to go out by vehicle		вы́ехать
приходи́ть		to come on foot [arrive]		прийти́
приезжа́ть		to come by vehicle [arrive]		прие́хать
заходи́ть		to drop in [visit] on foot		зайти́
заезжа́ть		to drop in [visit] by vehicle		зае́хать
	носи́ть	to carry on foot	нести́	
	вози́ть	to carry by vehicle	везти́	
приноси́ть		to bring on foot		принести́
привози́ть		to bring by vehicle		привезти́

идти́	
TO GO ON FOOT	
(SINGLE ACTION IN ONE DIRECTION)	
PRESENT TENSE	PAST TENSE
я иду́ ты идёшь он идёт мы идём вы идёте они́ иду́т	он шёл она́ шла оно́ шло они́ шли

ходи́ть	
TO GO ON FOOT	
(REPEATED ACTION)	
PRESENT TENSE	PAST TENSE
я хожу́ ты хо́дишь он хо́дит мы хо́дим вы хо́дите они́ хо́дят	Regular

е́хать	
TO GO BY VEHICLE	
(SINGLE ACTION IN ONE DIRECTION)	
PRESENT TENSE	PAST TENSE
я е́ду ты е́дешь он е́дет мы е́дем вы е́дете они́ е́дут	Regular

éздить	
TO GO BY VEHICLE	
(REPEATED ACTION)	
PRESENT TENSE	PAST TENSE
я éзжу	Regular
ты éздишь	
он éздит	
мы éздим	
вы éздите	
они éздят	

нести	
TO CARRY ON FOOT	
(SINGLE ACTION IN ONE DIRECTION)	
PRESENT TENSE	PAST TENSE
я несý	
ты несёшь	
он несёт	он нёс
мы несём	онá неслá
вы несёте	онó неслó
они несýт	они несли

носить	
TO CARRY ON FOOT	
(REPEATED ACTION)	
PRESENT TENSE	PAST TENSE
я ношý	Regular
ты нóсишь	
он нóсит	
мы нóсим	
вы нóсите	
они нóсят	

везти́
TO CARRY BY VEHICLE
(SINGLE ACTION IN ONE DIRECTION)

PRESENT TENSE	PAST TENSE
я везу́	
ты везёшь	
он везёт	он вёз
мы везём	она́ везла́
вы везёте	оно́ везло́
они́ везу́т	они́ везли́

вози́ть
TO CARRY BY VEHICLE
(REPEATED ACTION)

PRESENT TENSE	PAST TENSE
я вожу́	Regular
ты во́зишь	
он во́зит	
мы во́зим	
вы во́зите	
они́ во́зят	

QUIZ 17

In this quiz, or exercise, try to fill in the blanks with the proper form of "going" verbs, on foot or by vehicle, in one direction or denoting repeated action. Think carefully before choosing your answers.

1. Мы _____ сегóдня из Чикáго в Нью-Йóрк.	Today we came to New York from Chicago.
2. Я _____ в библиотéку кáждый деиь.	I go to the library every day.
3. Сегóдня он не _____ в библиотéку.	Today he is not going to the library.
4. Они́ _____ на дáчу кáждый год.	They go to the country every year.
5. В э́том годý они́ _____ к мóрю.	This year they are going to the seashore.
6. Я ви́дел её сегóдня, когдá онá _____ в шкóлу.	I saw her today when she was going to school.
7. Онá _____ с собóй две кни́ги.	She was carrying two books with her.
8. Нашá шкóла óчень далекó и мы должны́ _____ на автóбусе.	Our school is very far, and we have to [must] go by bus.

ANSWERS

1. прие́хали; 2. хожý; 3. идёт; 4. е́здят; 5. е́дут; 6. шла; 7. неслá; 8. е́здить.

B. In a Hotel

Здрáвствуйте. Мы тóлько что прие́хали из Нью-Йóрка.	Hello. We've just arrived from New York.
У вас есть свобóдные номерá?	Do you have any vacant [free] rooms?
Да, есть.	Yes, we do (have).
На какóм этажé э́ти номерá?	What floor are these rooms on?
На пя́том.	On the fifth.

Этот но́мер сли́шком тёмный.	This room is too dark.
На девя́том этаже́ есть но́мер, о́кна кото́рого выхо́дят на у́лицу.	On the ninth floor there is a room where the windows [the windows of which] face the street.
Мо́жно посмотре́ть?	May I see it? [Is it possible to look?]
Да, пожа́луйста.	Yes, please.
Этот но́мер мне о́чень нра́вится.	I like this room very much.
Пожа́луйста, принеси́те мо́й бага́ж (мои́ ве́щи) сюда́.	Please bring my baggage [my things] here.
Скажи́те, пожа́луйста, есть ли здесь парикма́херская?	Tell me, please, is there a barbershop here?
Парикма́херская–на второ́м этаже́.	The barbershop is on the second floor.
Она́ откры́та с девяти́ часо́в утра́ до пяти́ часо́в ве́чера.	It's open from nine in the morning to five o'clock in the afternoon.
А на како́м этаже́ пра́чечная?	And what floor is the laundry on?
Мне на́до погла́дить костю́м.	I have to have a suit pressed.
Пра́чечная на пя́том этаже́.	The laundry is on the fifth floor.
Кому́ мо́жно отда́ть бельё?	To whom should [may] I give my laundry?
Тут у меня́ не́сколько руба́шек и ни́жнее бельё.	I have [here] several shirts and some underwear.

Вы мо́жете отда́ть ва́ше бельё де́вушке, кото́рая убира́ет ва́шу ко́мнату.	You may turn in your laundry to the girl who cleans your room.
Когда́ оно́ бу́дет гото́во?	When will it be ready?
Бельё обы́чно гото́во че́рез два дня.	Laundry is usually ready in two days.
Э́то меня́ вполне́ устра́ивает.	That suits me completely.
А мо́жно заказа́ть за́втрак к себе́ в но́мер?	May I order break- fast in my room?
Коне́чно. На ка́ждом этаже́ есть своё обслу́живание.	Of course. Each floor has its own service.

SUPPLEMENTAL VOCABULARY 6: TRAVEL
AND TOURISM

tourist	тури́ст (m.)
hotel	оте́ль (m.)/ гости́ница (f.)
youth hostel	молодёжная гости́ница (f.)
reception desk	регистра́ция (f.)
to check in	зарегистри́роваться (imperf./perf.)
to check out	выпи́сываться - вы́писаться
reservation	бронь (f.), зака́з (m.)
passport	па́спорт (m.)
tour bus	туристи́ческий авто́бус (m.)
guided tour	экску́рсия (f.), на экску́рсии

camera	фотоаппарат (m.)
information center	информационный центр (m.)
map	карта (f.)
brochure	проспект (m.)
monument	памятник (m.)
to go sightseeing	осматривать – осмотреть достопримечательности (pl.)
to take a picture	фотографировать – сфотографировать
Can you take our picture?	Вы не могли бы нас сфотографировать ?

C. Imperfective and Perfective Forms of "To Give"

Imperfective (present)		Perfective (future)	
дава́ть		дать	
я даю́	I give	я дам	I will give
ты даёшь	you give	ты дашь	you will give
он даёт	he gives	он даст	he will give
мы даём	we give	мы дади́м	we will give
вы даёте	you give	вы дади́те	you will give
они́ даю́т	they give	они́ даду́т	they will give

от-дава́ть	to give out, away	от-да́ть
пере-дава́ть	to pass	пере-да́ть
за-дава́ть	to assign	за-да́ть
с-дава́ть	to deal (cards)	с-дать

D. In My Apartment

В ко́мнате стои́т стол и два сту́ла. На одно́й стене́ виси́т ка́рта го́рода, а на друго́й две

карти́ны. У меня́ в кварти́ре две ко́мнаты:
спа́льня и гости́ная. Гости́ная о́чень больша́я. В
гости́ной три окна́, и все выхо́дят на у́лицу. В
спа́льне то́лько одно́ окно́ во дво́р. Поэ́тому
в спа́льне о́чень ти́хо. В спа́льне стои́т больша́я
крова́ть, комо́д и шкаф для оде́жды.

There are a table and two chairs in the room. A map
of the city hangs on one wall, and two pictures on the
other. I have a one-bedroom apartment [I have two
rooms in my apartment]: a bedroom and a living room.
The living room is very big. In the living room there
are three windows, all of which face the street. There is
only one window in the bedroom, facing the courtyard.
Therefore, the bedroom is very quiet. In the bedroom
there is a large bed, a dresser, and a wardrobe.

Ку́хня ма́ленькая, но о́чень удо́бная. В ней
всё есть: и га́зовая плита́, и холоди́льник, и
мно́го по́лок и я́щиков для посу́ды. На окне́ в
ку́хне краси́вые ро́зовые занаве́ски.

The kitchen is small, but very comfortable. It is
fully equipped with [there is all (the equipment)] a gas
stove, a refrigerator, and a lot of shelves and drawers
for dishes. There are pretty pink curtains in the kitchen
window.

QUIZ 18

1. У вас есть свобо́дные
номера́?

a. The barbershop is on the
second floor.

2. Вы мо́жете отда́ть ва́ше
бельё сего́дня, и оно́
бу́дет гото́во за́втра.

b. Tell me, please, where the
barbershop is.

3. Э́то меня́ вполне́
устра́ивает.

c. I have to have a suit
pressed.

4. Óкна э́той ко́мнаты
   выхо́дят на у́лицу.

5. Скажи́те, пожа́луйста,
   где парикма́херская?

6. Парикма́херская–на
   второ́м этаже́.

7. Мы то́лько что
   прие́хали из Нью-Йо́рка.

8. Мне на́до погла́дить
   костю́м.

9. Пра́чечная на пя́том
   этаже́.

10. Офис откры́т с
    девяти́ часо́в утра́ до
    пяти́ часо́в ве́чера.

d. We've just arrived from
   New York.

e. The office is open from
   nine in the morning to five
   in the afternoon.

f. The tailor is on the fifth
   floor.

g. The windows of this room
   face the street.

h. Do you have any vacant
   [free] rooms?

i. This suits me completely.

j. You may turn in your
   laundry today, and it will
   be ready tomorrow.

ANSWERS

1—h; 2—j; 3—i; 4—g; 5—b; 6—a; 7—d; 8—c; 9—f; 10—e.

SUPPLEMENTAL VOCABULARY 7: AT HOME

house	дом (m.), дома (nom., pl.)
apartment	кварти́ра (f.)
room	ко́мната (f.)
living room	гости́ная (f.)
dining room	столо́вая (f.)
kitchen	ку́хня (f.)
bedroom	спа́льня (f.)
bathroom	ва́нная ко́мната (f.)
hall	холл (m.)
closet	шкаф (m.)
window	окно́ (n.)
door	дверь (f.)
table	стол (m.)
chair	стул (m.), сту́лья (nom., pl.), сту́льев (gen., pl.)

sofa/couch	диван (m.)
curtains	занавески (pl.)
carpet	ковер (m.)
television	телевидение (n.)
TV set	телевизор (m.)
cd player	cd [си-ди] проигрыватель (m.)
lamp	лампа (f.)
dvd player	dvd [ди-ви-ди] проигрыватель (m.)
sound system	музыкальный центр (m.)
painting/picture	картина (f.)
shelf	полка (f.)
stairs	лестница (f.)
ceiling	потолок (m.), потолки (nom., pl.)
wall	стена (f.)
floor	пол (m.)
big/small	большой/маленький
new/old	новый/старый
wood/wooden	дерево (n.)/деревянный
plastic/made from plastic	пластмасса (f.)/ пластмассовый

SUPPLEMENTAL VOCABULARY 8:
IN THE KITCHEN

refrigerator	холодильник (m.)
(kitchen) sink	(кухонная) раковина (f.)
counter	кухня (f.), кухонный стол (m.)
stove	плита (f.)
oven	духовка (f.)

microwave	микроволновая печь (f.), СВЧ [эс-вэ-че]
cupboard	буфет (m.)
drawer	ящик (m.)
plate	тарелка (f.)
cup	чашка (f.)
bowl	миска (f.)
glass	стакан (f.)
spoon	ложка (f.)
knife	нож (m.)
can	консервная банка (f.)
box	коробка (f.)
bottle	бутылка (f.)
carton	коробка (f.), пакет (m.)
coffee maker	кофеварка (f.)
tea kettle	чайник (m.)
blender	миксер (m.)
iron	утюг (m.)
ironing board	гладильная доска (f.)
broom	метла (f.), мётлы (nom., pl.)
dishwasher	посудомоечная машина (f.)
washing machine	стиральная машина (f.)
dryer	сушка (f.)
to cook	готовить – приготовить
to do the dishes	мыть – приготовить посуду (f.)
to do the laundry	стирать – постирать
dishwashing detergent	моющее средство (порошок (m.)) для посудомоечной машины
laundry detergent	стиральный порошок (m.), порошки

	(nom., pl.), моющее средство (n.)
bleach	отбеливатель (m.)
clean/dirty	чистый/грязный

SUPPLEMENTAL VOCABULARY 9:
IN THE BATHROOM

toilet	туалет (m.)
sink (wash basin)	раковина (f.)
bath tub	ванна (f.)
shower	душ (m.)
mirror	зеркало (n.)
medicine cabinet	аптечка (f.) (not common in Russian bathrooms)
towel	полотенце (n.)
toilet paper	туалетная бумага (f.)
shampoo	шампунь (m.)
soap	мыло (n.)
bath gel	гель (m.) для душа
shaving cream	крем (m.), кремы (nom., pl.) для бритья
razor	бритва (f.)
to wash oneself	мыться – помыться, вымыться
to take a shower/bath	принимать душ/ванну
to shave	бриться – побриться
cologne	одеколон (m.) (для мужчин)
perfume	духи (pl.) (для женщин)
deodorant	дезодорант (m.)
bandage	пластырь (m.)
powder	пудра (f.)

LESSON 28

A. In a Restaurant

Максим:
**Вот, здесь о́коло окна́
хоро́ший сто́лик.**

Пётр:
**О́чень хорошо́.
Я о́чень люблю́
смотре́ть в окно́.**

Максим:
**Дава́йте посмо́трим,
что сего́дня на обе́д.
Бара́нина жа́реная,
бифште́кс
натура́льный
и́ли бифште́кс
ру́бленый. Бли́нчики
с мя́сом. Суп из
све́жих овоще́й.
Карто́фельное пюре́.**

Пётр:
**Зна́ете, что я возьму́?
Я хочу́ хоро́шей
ры́бы.
Я о́чень люблю́ ры́бу,
и говоря́т, что здесь
её великоле́пно
гото́вят. На десе́рт
я возьму́ компо́т из
сухофру́ктов.**

Максим:
**А я бу́ду мясны́е
котле́ты и
моро́женое на десе́рт.**

Maxim:
Look, here's a good
table near the window.

Peter:
Very good. I like to
look out the window.

Maxim:
Let's see what they
have for dinner
today. Lamb chops,
regular steak or
chopped sirloin.
Blinchiki with meat.
Fresh vegetable soup.
Mashed potatoes.

Peter:
You know what I'll
have? I want some
good fish. I love
fish, and they say that
they prepare it very
well here. For dessert
I'll have a compote
of dried fruit.

Maxim:
And I'll have meat
cutlets, and ice cream
for dessert.

Пётр:	*Peter:*
Официáнт! Пожáлуйста принесúте нам бутьíлочку винá. Какóго-нибýдь харóшего грузинского.	Waiter! Please bring us a bottle of wine. Some good wine from Georgia.
Максúм:	*Maxim:*
Ах, какóе замечáтельное винó. Ну, за вáше здорóвье, мой дорогóй друг!	Ah! What excellent wine. Well, to your health, my dear friend!
Пётр:	*Peter:*
И за вáше тóже! Тепéрь нýжно закусúть. Вот кусóчек сьíра. Éшьте, пожáлуйста. Ах, как вкýсно!	And to yours also! Now we must eat a bit. Here's a piece of cheese. Please have some. Oh, how delicious!
Максúм:	*Maxim:*
Ну, ещё по бокáлу. За мир, и счáстье всех людéй во всём мúре.	Let's each have another glass. To peace, and to the happiness of all people in the whole world.
Пётр:	*Peter:*
Ну, знáете, за такóй тост нельзя́ не вьíпить.	Well, you know, it's impossible not to drink to such a toast.
Максúм:	*Maxim:*
Ну, ещё одúн бокáл?	Well, another glass?
Пётр:	*Peter:*
Нет, спасúбо, я бóльше не хочý.	No, thank you, I don't want any more.
Максúм:	*Maxim:*
Ну, ещё по бокáлу.	Just one more!

Пётр:	*Peter:*
Нет, я сказáл ужé, что бóльше не хочý, и бóльше не бýду. Давáйте есть.	No, I already said that I don't want any more and won't drink any more. Let's eat.

Максим:	*Maxim:*
Ну, ничегó с вáми не подéлаешь. Давáйте есть. А я вы́пил бы ещё.	Well, if I can't do anything [nothing can be done] with you . . . Let's eat. But I would have had another [drunk another].

Пётр:	*Peter:*
Вы пéйте, а я бóльше не хочý.	You drink, but I don't want any more.

Максим:	*Maxim:*
Официáнт! Скóлько мы вам должны́?	Waiter! How much do we owe you?

B. FOOD AND UTENSILS

мáсло	butter
хлеб	bread
соль	salt
пéрец	pepper
салáт	salad, lettuce
подли́вка	sauce, gravy
зéлень	green vegetables, herbs
óвощи	vegetables
стакáн воды́	glass of water
чай	tea
кóфе	coffee
фрýкты	fruit
холóдная закýска	hors d'oeuvres

второе блюдо	main course
сладкое	sweet course
десерт	dessert
нож	knife
столовая ложка	tablespoon or soup spoon
чайная ложечка	teaspoon
тарелка	plate
тарелочка	small plate
глубокая тарелка	soup bowl
блюдо	platter
чашка	cup
блюдце	saucer
стакан	glass
салфетка	napkin
солонка	salt shaker

C.   MORE: USE OF Ещё OR Больше

The word "more" can be expressed in Russian by either ещё or больше.

Вы хотите ещё чаю?	Do you want some more tea?
Нет, я больше не хочу.	No, I don't want any more.
Да, я хочу ещё.	Yes, I want (some) more.
Я приду к вам ещё раз.	I will come to you once more.
Я больше к вам не буду приходить.	I will not come to you any more.

It is generally true that to express "more" affirmatively, ещё is used; to say "no more" or "I don't want more," or when "more" is coupled with any negative verb, бо́льше is used.

Я хочу́ ещё.	I want more.
Он бо́льше не хо́чет.	He doesn't want more.
Я хочу́ ещё чита́ть.	I want to read some more.
Она́ вас бо́льше не лю́бит.	She doesn't love you any more.

D. CONJUGATION OF "TO EAT"

ЕСТЬ	TO EAT
я ем	I eat
ты ешь	you eat
он ест	he eats
мы еди́м	we eat
вы еди́те	you eat
они едя́т	they eat
PAST TENSE	
он ел	he
она́ е́ла	she ate
оно́ е́ло	it ate
они́ е́ли	they ate

QUIZ 19

1. Пожа́луйста, принеси́те бути́лочку вина́.
2. Нет, я бо́льше не хочу́.
3. Нет, я ещё не ко́нчил.
4. Я о́чень люблю́ ры́бу.
5. Я ещё не ел ры́бу в э́том рестора́не.

a. I can't eat any [thing] more.
b. He doesn't want any more meat.
c. Because I am not hungry anymore.
d. There is no more compote.

6. Он бо́льше не хо́чет мя́са. e. Do you want anything else?

7. Почему́ вы бо́льше не хоти́те? f. No, I don't want any more.

8. Потому́ что я бо́льше не го́лоден. g. Please bring a bottle of wine.

9. Я не ем, потому́ что я ещё не го́лоден. h. I like fish very much.

i. I haven't eaten fish yet in this restaurant.

10. На десе́рт я возьму́ компо́т из сухофру́ктов. j. No, thanks, I am finished.

11. Компо́та бо́льше нет. k. No, I haven't finished yet.

12. Вы хоти́те ещё что́-нибудь? l. Too bad. As for me, I would have had another.

13. Нет, спаси́бо, я уже́ ко́нчил. m. For dessert I'll have compote of dried fruit.

14. Я бо́льше ничего́ не могу́ съесть. n. Why don't you want any more?

15. Жаль. А я бы вы́пил ещё. o. I'm not eating because I'm not hungry yet.

ANSWERS

1—g; 2—f; 3—k; 4—h; 5—i; 6—b; 7—n; 8—c; 9—o; 10—m; 11—d; 12—e; 13—j; 14—a; 15—l.

SUPPLEMENTAL VOCABULARY 10: FOOD

dinner (early evening meal, supper)	ужин (m.)
lunch(early afternoon meal)	ланч (m.), обед
breakfast	завтрак (m.)
meat	мясо (n.)
chicken	курица (f.)
beef	говядина (f.)
pork	свинина (f.)
fish	рыба (f.)
shrimp	креветки (pl.)
lobster	омар (m.)
bread	хлеб (m.)

egg	яйцо (n.), яйца (nom., pl.)
cheese	сыр (m.)
rice	рис (m.)
vegetable	овощ (m.)
lettuce	салат (m.)
tomato	помидор (m.)
carrot	морковь (f.) (sg.)
cucumber	огурец (m.), огурцы (nom., pl.)
pepper	перец (m.), перцы (nom., pl.)
fruit	фрукт (m.)
apple	яблоко (n.), яблоки (nom., pl.)
orange	апельсин (m.)
banana	банан (m.)
pear	груша (f.)
grapes	виноград (m.) (sg.)
drink	напиток (m.), напитки (nom., pl.)
water	вода (f.) (sg.)
milk	молоко (n.) (sg.)
juice	сок (m.)
coffee	кофе (m.)
tea	чай (m.)
wine	вино (n.)
beer	пиво (n.)
soft drink/soda	безалкогольный напиток (m.)/ газировка (f.)/ газированная вода
salt	соль (f.)
sugar	сахар (m.)
honey	мёд (m.)
hot/cold	горячий/холодный
sweet/sour	сладкий/кислый

LESSON 29

A. MORE ON PERFECTIVE AND IMPERFECTIVE VERBS

This lesson provides further examples of the use of perfective and imperfective verbs.

Мы бу́дем писа́ть пи́сьма.   писа́ть
We will write letters.

Я напишу́ письмо́.   написа́ть
I will write (start and finish) the letter.

Я бу́ду опи́сывать всё.   опи́сывать
I will describe everything over time.

Брат опи́шет вы́ставку.   описа́ть
(My) brother will describe the exhibition (completely).

Он встаёт ра́но ка́ждый   встава́ть
день.
He gets up early every day [imperfective].

Вчера́ он встал о́чень   встать
по́здно.
Yesterday he got up very late [once, completed: perfective].

За́втра он вста́нет . . .   встать
Tomorrow he will be getting up [one time: perfective] . . .

Ле́том он бу́дет встава́ть . . .   встава́ть
During the summer he will get up [every day: imperfective future] . . .

Я забы́л бума́жник до́ма.   забы́ть
I forgot my wallet at home [this one time: perfective past].

Он всегда́ всё забыва́ет.   забыва́ть
He always forgets everything [all the time: imperfective].

Он всё де́лает о́чень   де́лать
бы́стро.
He does everything very quickly [everything, all the time: imperfective].

Он сде́лает э́то за́втра.   сде́лать
He will do this tomorrow [one time, tomorrow: perfective future].

B.   SAMPLE SENTENCES: DAILY ACTIVITIES

Éсли за́втра бу́дет хоро́шая пого́да, я пойду́ гуля́ть в парк.	If the weather is good tomorrow, I will go to the park for a walk.
Ве́чером я бу́ду сиде́ть до́ма.	I'll stay home in the evening.
Мой брат то́же бу́дет до́ма за́втра.	My brother will also be home tomorrow.
Мы бу́дем писа́ть пи́сьма роди́телям.	We'll write letters to our parents.

Я напишу́ письмо́ моему́ дру́гу.	I'll write a letter to my friend.
Брат напи́шет письмо́ сестре́ в Ме́ксику.	(My) brother will write a letter to (our) sister in Mexico.
Я бу́ду опи́сывать всё, что мы ви́дели в Москве́.	I'll describe everything we saw in Moscow.
Брат опи́шет худо́жественную вы́ставку.	(My) brother will describe the art exhibition.
За́втра у́тром мы пойдём в музе́й.	Tomorrow morning we'll go to the museum.
По доро́ге мы зайдём за мои́м дру́гом.	On the way we'll drop by to pick up my friend.
Он бу́дет нас ждать.	He'll wait for us.
Пусть подождёт. Я жда́ла его́ мно́го раз!	Let him wait. I've waited for him many times!
Я бы́стро помо́юсь, оде́нусь и причешу́сь.	I'll wash (myself), dress (myself), and comb my hair quickly.
Я всегда́ бы́стро мо́юсь, одева́юсь и причёсываюсь.	I always wash (myself), dress (myself), and comb my hair quickly.
Он встаёт ра́но ка́ждый день.	He gets up [rises] early every day.
Вчера́ он встал о́чень по́здно.	Yesterday he got up very late.
За́втра он вста́нет, как всегда́, ра́но.	Tomorrow he will get up early, as always.
Ле́том он бу́дет встава́ть в во́семь часо́в.	In the summer he will be getting up at eight o'clock.

Скажи́те ему́, что я бу́ду у него́ за́втра.

Tell him that I'll be at his house [by him] tomorrow.

C. More Verb Practice

Он всегда́ всё забыва́ет.

He always forgets everything.

По́езд отхо́дит в два часа́.

The train leaves at two o'clock.

Сего́дня он отойдёт в три часа́.

Today it will leave at three o'clock.

По́езд отошёл во́время.

The train left on time.

Вы говори́те сли́шком бы́стро. Я вас не понима́ю.

You talk too fast. I don't understand you.

Е́сли вы ска́жете всё э́то ме́дленно, я вас пойму́.

If you say all that slowly, I'll understand you.

Мы прочтём меню́ и пото́м зака́жем обе́д.

We'll read the menu and then order dinner.

Официа́нт ско́ро принесёт суп.

The waiter will bring the soup soon.

Я не могу́ бо́льше ждать.

I can't wait any longer.

Он смо́жет э́то сде́лать, е́сли полу́чит всё, что ему́ ну́жно.

He'll be able to do that if he gets everything he needs.

QUIZ 20

1. За́втра у́тром мы _____ в музе́й.

Tomorrow morning we'll go to the museum.

2. Я всегда́
   бы́стро _____.

   I always wash
   (myself) quickly.

3. Я бы́стро _____
   и _____ в шко́лу.

   I'll wash (myself)
   quickly and go to
   school.

4. Он _____ ра́но
   ка́ждый день.

   He gets up early
   every day.

5. За́втра он _____.
   как всегда́, ра́но.

   Tomorrow he will
   get up early, as usual.

6. Ле́том он _____
   в во́семь часо́в.

   In the summer he
   will be getting up at
   eight o'clock.

7. Е́сли вы _____
   всё э́то ме́дленно,
   я вас пойму́.

   If you say all
   that slowly, I will (be
   able to) understand
   you.

8. Официа́нт ско́ро _____
   суп.

   The waiter will bring the
   soup soon.

9. По́езд _____
   во́время.

   The train left on
   time.

10. Я не могу́ _____
    ждать.

    I can't wait any
    longer.

ANSWERS

1. пойдём; 2. мо́юсь; 3. помо́юсь, пойду́; 4. встаёт; 5. вста́нет;
6. бу́дет встава́ть; 7. ска́жете; 8. принесёт; 9. отошёл; 10.
бо́льше.

LESSON 30

A. INTRODUCTIONS

Кто там?

Who's there?

Мо́жно войти́?

May I come
in?

Входи́те, пожа́луйста.

Please come in.

**Позво́льте вам
   предста́вить моего́
   дру́га.**

Allow me to introduce
   my friend to you.

Óчень рад с вáми познакóмиться.	I'm very glad to meet you [to become acquainted with you].
Óчень приятно.	Delighted. [Very pleasant.]
Разрешите предстáвиться.	Allow me to introduce myself.
Меня зовýт Ивáн Петрóвич Крылóв.	My name is [they call me] Ivan Petrovich Krilov.
Садитесь, пожáлуйста.	Please have a seat.
Мóжно вам предложить чáю?	May I offer you some tea?
Вы хотите со мной поговорить?	You want to speak with me?
Что вам нýжно?	What do you need?

B.   AT THE TRAIN STATION

Скажите мне, пожáлуйста, где вокзáл?	Please tell me where the train station is.
Идите пря́мо до углá, потóм налéво один квартáл.	Go straight to the corner, then one block to the left.
Где продаю́т билéты?	Where do they sell tickets?
Вон там кáсса.	There's the ticket office.
Бóже мой! Какáя большáя óчередь!	Good heavens! What a long line!
Не беспокóйтесь.	Don't worry.
Óчередь идёт óчень быстро.	The line moves quickly.
Дáйте мне, пожáлуйста, билéт в Я́сную Поля́ну.	Please give me a ticket to Yasnaya Polyana.

Вам в одну́ сто́рону и́ли туда́ и обра́тно?	Do you want a one-way ticket or a round trip?
Туда́ и обра́тно, пожа́луйста.	Round trip, please.
Когда́ отхо́дит по́езд? Да́йте мне, пожа́луйста, расписа́ние поездо́в.	When does the train leave? Give me a timetable, please.
Поезда́ в Я́сную Поля́ну отхо́дят ка́ждый час.	Trains to Yasnaya Polyana leave every hour.
Где аэропо́рт?	Where is the airport?
Аэропо́рт о́чень далеко́.	The airport is very far away.
Туда́ ну́жно е́хать и́ли на авто́бусе, и́ли на такси́.	You have to take a bus or a taxi to get there.
Вот э́ти такси́ е́дут то́лько в аэропо́рт.	[Here] these taxis go only to the airport.
Туда́ по кра́йней ме́ре полчаса́ езды́.	It's at least a half-hour trip.
В аэропорту́, пре́жде чем сесть на самолёт, ну́жно получи́ть поса́дочный тало́н.	At the airport you have to get a boarding pass before you can get on the plane.
Пойдёмте! Уже́ о́чень по́здно.	Let's go. It's very late already.
Я не люблю́ опа́здывать.	I don't like to be late.
Э́то такси́ свобо́дно?	Is this taxi available?
Нам ну́жно в аэропо́рт.	We have to go to the airport.
Сади́тесь, пожа́луйста!	Get in, please.

C. In Case of Illness

Есть ли здесь в гости́нице врач?	Is there a doctor in the hotel?
У меня́ о́чень боли́т голова́ и го́рло.	I have a bad headache and sore throat.
У меня́ на́сморк.	I have a head cold.
У меня́ боля́т зу́бы.	I have a toothache.
У него́ боли́т спина́.	His back hurts.
У неё температу́ра (жар).	She has a fever.
Нет ли у вас слаби́тельного?	Do you have a laxative?
Я о́чень пло́хо сплю.	I sleep very poorly.
Глаза́, у́ши, го́рло, нос, грудь, бок, ру́ки, но́ги; па́льцы на рука́х, па́льцы на нога́х.	Eyes, ears, throat, nose, chest (breast), side, hands (arms), feet (legs), fingers, toes.
Голова́ кру́жится.	I am dizzy [my head is spinning].
У вас температу́ра.	You have a fever.
Боли́т живо́т.	My stomach aches.
Боль в желу́дке.	A pain in the stomach.
Мне ну́жно лежа́ть в посте́ли?	Do I have to stay in bed?
Да, обяза́тельно.	Yes, definitely.
Меня́ тошни́т.	I am nauseous.
Принима́йте э́то лека́рство четы́ре ра́за в день по столо́вой ло́жке.	Take a tablespoon of this medicine four times a day.
Но́чью сде́лайте себе́ согрева́ющий компре́сс.	At night apply a hot compress.

Ну́жно ли полоска́ть го́рло, до́ктор?	Should I gargle, doctor?
Да. Возьми́те одну́ ча́йную ло́жку со́ли на стака́н горя́чей воды́ и полощи́те по кра́йней ме́ре три ра́за в день: ка́ждые четы́ре часа́.	Yes. Add one teaspoon of salt to a glass of hot water and gargle at least three times a day, every four hours.
Не выходи́те, пока́ у вас не бу́дет норма́льная температу́ра.	Don't go out until your temperature is normal.

QUIZ 21

1. Мо́жно вам предложи́ть ча́ю?
2. Меня́ зову́т Ива́н Крыло́в.
3. Скажи́те мне, пожа́луйста, где вокза́л?
4. Бо́же мой! Кака́я больша́я о́чередь!
5. Ива́н Крыло́в хорошо́ зна́ет го́род.
6. Вам в одну́ сто́рону или туда́ и обра́тно?
7. Поезда́ отхо́дят ка́ждый час.
8. Туда́ по кра́йней ме́ре полчаса́ езды́.
9. Я не люблю́ опа́здывать.
10. Не беспоко́йтесь, о́чередь идёт о́чень бы́стро.

a. Ivan Krilov knows the city well.
b. I don't like to be late.
c. Do you want a one-way or a round-trip (ticket)?
d. May I offer you some tea?
e. My name is Ivan Krilov.
f. It's at least a half-hour trip.
g. Don't worry. The line is moving quickly.
h. Please tell me where the train station is.
i. Trains leave every hour.
j. Good heavens! What a long line!

ANSWERS

1—d; 2—e; 3—h; 4—j; 5—a; 6—c; 7—i; 8—f; 9—b; 10—g.

SUPPLEMENTAL VOCABULARY II:
THE HUMAN BODY

head	голова (f.)
face	лицо (n.)
forehead	лоб (m.), лбы (nom., pl.)
eye	глаз (m.), глаза (nom., pl.)
eyebrow	бровь (f.)
eyelash	ресница (f.)
ear	ухо (n.), уши (nom., pl.)
nose	нос (m.)
mouth	рот (m.), рты (nom., pl.)
tooth	зуб (m.)
tongue	язык (m.)
cheek	щека (f.)
chin	подбородок (m.), подбородки (nom., pl.)
hair	волосы (pl.)
neck	шея (f.)
chest	грудь (f.)
breast	грудь (f.)
shoulders	плечи (pl.)
arm	рука (f.)
elbow	локоть (m.), локти (nom., pl.)
wrist	запястье (n.) (formal)
hand	рука (f.) (colloquially, it refers to all of its parts)
stomach/abdomen	желудок (m.)/брюшная полость (f.) (formal), живот (m.) (coll.)
penis	пенис (m.) (formal)
vagina	влагалище (n.) (formal)

leg	нога (f.) (colloquially, it refers to all parts of the limb)
knee	колено (n.), колени (nom., pl.)
ankle	щиколотка (f.)
foot	ступня (f.)
finger	палец (m.), пальцы
toe	палец на ноге
skin	кожа (f.)
blood	кровь (f.)
brain	мозг (m.)
heart	сердце (n.)
lungs	лёгкие (pl.)
bone	кость (f.)
muscle	мышца (f.)
tendon	сухожилие (n.)

LESSON 31

A. MOSCOW THEATRES

Иван:
Éсли бы я знал, что сегóдня идёт в москóвских теáтрах, я бы пошёл в теáтр.

Ivan:
If I knew what's playing in the Moscow theatres today, I would go to the theatre.

Вéра:
Есть такáя мáленькая кни́жечка, котóрая называ́ется «Репертуáр москóвских теáтров».

Vera:
There is a small book called *Program [Repertoire] of the Moscow Theatres.*

Иван:
Где её мóжно купи́ть?

Ivan:
Where can one buy it?

Вéра:
**Во всех
театра́льных кáссах.**

Vera:
At all box offices.

Ивáн:
**Éсли бы я знал э́то
рáньше, то давно́
бы купи́л её.**

Ivan:
If I had known that
before [earlier], I
would have bought it
a long time ago.

Вéра:
**Ну, вот ви́дите. Всё
узнаётся в своё
врéмя.**

Vera:
There, you see. In
time one learns every-
thing.

Ивáн:
**В Москвé мнóго
теáтров?**

Ivan:
Are there many the-
atres in Moscow?

Вéра:
**Да! Óчень мнóго!
Давáйте посмóтрим.
Вот Большо́й теáтр.
Там иду́т óперы и
балéт.**

Vera:
Yes. Very many. Let's
look (at the book).
Here is the Bolshoi
Theatre. Operas and
ballet play there.

Ивáн:
Где он нахóдится?

Ivan:
Where is it?

Вéра:
**На Театрáльной
плóщади. Потóм
есть филиáл Боль-
шо́го теáтра, на
Пу́шкинской улице.
Э́то тóже óперный
теáтр.**

Vera:
On Theatre Square.
Then there's an affili-
ate of the Bolshoi
Theatre on Pushkin
Street. This is also an
opera theatre.

Ивáн:
**А где нахóдится
Москóвский
Худóжественный
теáтр?**

Ivan:
And where is the
Moscow Art Theatre?

Ве́ра:
**На про́езде
Худо́жественного
Теа́тра. Там иду́т
то́лько дра́мы и
коме́дии. Пото́м есть
Ма́лый теа́тр, теа́тр
и́мени Вахта́нгова,
теа́тр Опере́тты
и т.д., и т.д.**

Vera:
On Art Theatre Lane.
Only dramas and
comedies play there.
Then there's the
Maliy Theatre, the
theatre named after
Vahktangov, the
Theatre of Operetta,
etc., etc.

Ива́н:
**В Москве́ есть
цирк?**

Ivan:
Is there a circus in
Moscow?

Ве́ра:
**Ещё бы! Коне́чно
есть. И како́й
замеча́тельный!
Обяза́тельно
пойди́те в цирк.
Ста́рый цирк
нахо́дится на
Цветно́м бульва́ре,
дом 13. А но́вое
зда́ние ци́рка на
проспе́кте Верна́д-
ского. А мо́жно
ли доста́ть биле́ты
на сего́дня, я не
зна́ю. Ну́жно
позвони́ть им по
телефо́ну. Вот их
но́мер: 212-16-40.**

Vera:
And then some! Of course
there is! And what an
excellent one! Go to
the circus without fail.
The old circus is
on Flower Boulevard,
No. 13. But the new
circus building is on
Vernadsky Prospect.
I don't know if it's
possibly to get tickets
for today. You should
(it is necessary to)
call them (on the tele-
phone). Here's their
number: 212-16-40.

Ива́н:
**Алло́, алло́. Ска-
жи́те, пожа́луйста,**

Ivan:
Hello, hello. Do you.
have tickets for today?

есть биле́ты на се-
го́дня? Нет? Почему?
Ах, у вас сего́дня
выходно́й. Как
жаль . . . Сего́дня нет
представле́ния.
Ну, вот ви́дите как
мне везёт.

No? Why? Oh, you're
closed today [today is
your day off]. What a
pity . . . There's no performance today. There,
you see; that's my luck.

Ве́ра:
Вы мо́жете пойти́
за́втра.

Vera:
You can go tomorrow.

Ива́н:
Нет, я уже́
не успе́ю.

Ivan:
No, I won't have
time.

Ве́ра:
Почему́? Ра́зве вы
ско́ро уезжа́ете?

Vera:
Why? Are you leaving
soon?

Ива́н:
Коне́чно. За́втра. Ах,
е́сли бы я зна́л об
э́том ра́ньше, е́сли
бы мне сказа́ли э́то
хотя́ бы неде́лю тому́
наза́д!

Ivan:
Of course. Tomorrow.
Ah, if I had known
about this earlier, if
someone had told me
that at least a week
ago!

Ве́ра:
Е́сли бы я зна́ла, что
вы ничего́ не зна́ете,
я бы сказа́ла вам.

Vera:
If I had known that
you didn't know any-
thing, I would have
told you.

Ива́н:
Вы же зна́ете, что я
не ме́стный! Отку́да
же мне знать?

Ivan:
But you know that
I'm not a local! How
am I to know?

Ве́ра:
Ну, прости́те. Ну, не
серди́тесь!

Vera:
Oh, well, forgive me.
Now, don't be angry!

Ива́н:
**Я не сержу́сь. Но
мне всё же о́чень,
о́чень жаль, что я
не побыва́л в ци́рке.
Я так люблю́ цирк.**

Ivan:
I'm not angry. But all
the same I'm very,
very sorry that I
didn't get to the cir-
cus. I just love the
circus.

Ве́ра:
**Ну, ничего́. В
сле́дующий раз.**

Vera:
Well, that's okay.
Next time.

B. SUBJUNCTIVE AND CONDITIONAL MOODS

The conditional and subjunctive are likely to be
among the most difficult grammatical constructions in
any language. However, in Russian, they are the easiest. All you have to know is the particle бы, and that
the past tense of the verb is used together with it.

е́сли бы	if
Если бы я знал,	If I knew,
	Had I known,
я пошёл бы.	I would have gone.
	I would go.
Я позвони́л бы,	I would have called you,
е́сли бы у меня́ был	if I had your telephone
(бы) ваш телефо́н.	number.

C. WORD STUDY

просто́й	simple
взро́слый	adult
гость	guest
рубль	ruble
назва́ние	title
приглаша́ть-пригласи́ть	to invite

не́сколько	several
открыва́ть-откры́ть	to open
у́жин	supper
у́тро	morning

QUIZ 22

1. Ну, вот ви́дите. Всё узнаётся в своё вре́мя.

2. Почему́? Ра́зве вы ско́ро уезжа́ете?

3. Сего́дня нет представле́ния.

4. Е́сли бы я знал э́то ра́ньше, то давно́ бы купи́л её.

5. О́чень мно́го. Дава́йте посмо́трим.

6. Он о́чень хорошо́ говори́т по-ру́сски.

7. В на́шем го́роде есть замеча́тельный цирк.

8. Где он нахо́дится?

9. Я о́чень люблю́ цирк и хожу́ туда́ о́чень ча́сто.

10. Моя́ сестра́ живёт и рабо́тает в ма́леньком го́роде.

11. Два дня тому́ наза́д я был в теа́тре.

12. В Моско́вском Худо́жественном теа́тре иду́т дра́мы и коме́дии.

13. А мно́го теа́тров в Москве́?

14. Он никогда́ ничего́ не зна́ет.

15. Она́ не зна́ла, что сего́дня э́тот магази́н закры́т.

a. He speaks Russian very well.

b. Are there many theatres in Moscow?

c. Where is it located?

d. I really love the circus and go there often.

e. I was at the theatre two days ago.

f. He never knows anything.

g. Tell me, please, is it possible to get tickets for today?

h. There, you see; that's my luck.

i. There's no performance today.

j. Oh, well, forgive me. Now, don't be annoyed!

k. There, you see. In time one learns everything.

l. Very many. Let's take a look.

m. She didn't know that this store is closed today.

n. We have an excellent circus in our town.

o. If I had known that before [earlier], I would have bought it a long time ago.

16. Скажи́те, пожа́луйста, мо́жно ли купи́ть биле́ты на сего́дня?	p. You can go tomorrow.
17. Ну, вот ви́дите, как мне везёт.	q. Dramas and comedies play at the Moscow Art Theatre.
18. Вы мо́жете пойти́ за́втра.	r. My sister lives and works in a small town.
19. Ну, прости́те. Ну, не серди́тесь!	s. Well, that's okay. Next time.
20. Ну, ничего́. В сле́дующий раз.	t. Why? Are you leaving soon?

NOTE

Quizzes from this point on will include review sentences from previous lessons.

ANSWERS

1—k; 2—t; 3—i; 4—o; 5—l; 6—a; 7—n; 8—c; 9—d; 10—r; 11—e; 12—q; 13—b; 14—f; 15—m; 16—g; 17—h; 18—p; 19—j; 20—s.

LESSON 32

A. USEFUL WORDS AND EXPRESSIONS

Вот как!	Is that so!
Как бы не так!	Nothing of the sort!
Бу́дьте как до́ма!	Make yourself at home.
как ви́дно	as can be seen
Э́то как раз то, что мне ну́жно.	That's just what I need.
Э́то де́ло вку́са.	That's a matter of taste.
Соверше́нно ве́рно.	Quite right. [Absolutely.]
Ещё бы.	And how! You bet!

ко́е-как	anyhow; haphazardly
Он холосто́й.	He's a bachelor.
Он же́нится.	He is getting married.
Он жена́т.	He is married.
Она́ ещё не за́мужем.	She is still not married.
Она́ выхо́дит за́муж.	She is getting married.
Она́ за́мужем.	She is married.
(родно́й) брат	brother
(родна́я) сестра́	sister
двою́родный брат	(first) cousin (*m.*)
двою́родная сестра́	(first) cousin (*f.*)
смотре́ть в о́ба	keep one's eyes open: be on one's guard
Э́тому не помо́жешь.	It can't be helped.
пока́ что	in the meantime
Поговори́те с ним, пока́ он там.	Talk to [with] him while he is there.
Оста́вьте меня́ в поко́е.	Leave me alone [in peace].
Он про́сто ничего́ не зна́ет.	He simply knows nothing.
Он ничего́ не име́ет про́тив э́того.	He has nothing against it. [He doesn't mind.]
Она́ лю́бит пуска́ть пыль в глаза́.	She likes to show off [to put on airs].
Тру́дно рабо́тать на пусто́й желу́док.	It's difficult to work on an empty stomach.
Нам с ва́ми по пути́.	We're going your way.
У вас золото́е се́рдце.	You have a heart of gold.
Благодарю́ вас от всего́ се́рдца.	Thank you from the bottom of my heart.
С глаз доло́й, из се́рдца вон.	Out of sight, out of mind.
бежа́ть изо все́х сил	to run as fast as one can

кричáть изо всéх сил	to scream at the top
кричáть во всё гóрло	of one's voice
Он дéлает э́то по привы́чке.	He does it out of habit.
лéгче сказáть, чем сдéлать	easier said than done
скáзано–сдéлано	no sooner said than done
в скóром врéмени	before long
скóрая пóмощь	first aid
одни́м слóвом	in a word; in short
други́ми словáми	in other words
Всё бýдет забы́то.	Everything will be forgotten.
глáвным óбразом	mainly
таки́м óбразом	in this way
на вся́кий слýчай	just in case
во вся́ком слýчае	in any case
в такóм слýчае	in this case

B. TELEPHONE CALLS

Откýда мóжно позвони́ть?	Where can I make a phone call?
Здесь есть телефóн-автомáт?	Is there a payphone here?
Здесь есть телефóнный спрáвочник?	Is there a telephone directory?
Я хочý позвони́ть по э́тому нóмеру.	I'd like to call this number.
Я хочý позвони́ть в Соединённые Штáты.	I'd like to call the United States.
Аллó.	Hello.
Говори́т …	This is …

Кто звони́т?	Who is calling?
С кем я говорю́?	To whom am I speaking?
Говори́те ме́дленно, пожа́луйста.	Speak slowly, please.
Э́то Андре́й.	This is Andrei.
Мо́жно поговори́ть с Ва́димом?	May I speak with Vadim?
Мой но́мер ...	My number is ...
Как мне связа́ться с опера́тором?	How do I get the operator?
Меня́ разъедини́ли.	I was cut off.
Вы могли́ бы соедини́ть меня́ ещё раз?	Could you connect me again?
Я хоте́л бы поговори́ть с ...	I'd like to speak to ...
Скажи́те ему́, пожа́луйста, что я звони́л.	Please tell him I called.

C. FAXES, E-MAIL, INTERNET, COMPUTERS

Мне ну́жно посла́ть факс.	I have to send a fax.
У вас есть факс?	Do you have a fax machine?
Я вам пошлю́ об э́том сообще́ние по электро́нной по́чте.	I'll send you an e-mail about it.
У вас есть до́ступ к Интерне́ту?	Do you have an Internet connection?
Мне ну́жно посмотре́ть на Интерне́те.	I need to do some research on the Web.
Мне понра́вился ваш сайт.	I like your website.

У вас есть электронная страница.	Do you have a webpage!
У меня завис компьютер.	My computer is down.
Какого объёма ваш жёсткий диск?	How big is your hard drive?
Я собираюсь сделать апгрейд моего компьютера (coll.)./ Я собираюсь модернизировать мой компьютер.	I'm thinking of upgrading my computer.

D. Word Study

забыва́ть-забы́ть	to forget
пра́здник	holiday
оши́бка	mistake
хо́лодно	cold (adv.)
гру́стный	sad
прекра́сный	wonderful
хлеб	bread
остано́вка	stop
дверь	door

SUPPLEMENTAL VOCABULARY 12: COMPUTERS AND THE INTERNET

computer	компью́тер (m.)
keyboard	клавиату́ра (f.)
monitor/screen	монито́р (m.)/экра́н (m.)
printer	при́нтер (m.)
mouse	мы́шка (f.)
modem	моде́м (m.)

memory	память (f.)
cd rom	компьютерный диск (m.)
cd rom drive	дисковод (m.)
file	файл (m.)
document	документ (m.)
cable (dsl)	кабель (m.) dsl [ди-эс-эл]/ отдельного подключения
internet	Интернет (m.)
website	вэб сайт (m.)
web page	вэб страница (m.)
e-mail	электронная почта (f.), сообщение (n.) (message)
chat room	чат
web log (blog)	вэб форум (m.)
attachment	вложенный файл (m.)
to send an e-mail	посылать – послать сообщение (n.)
to send a file	посылать – послать файл (m.)
to forward	пересылать – переслать
to reply	отвечать – ответить
to delete	удалять – удалить
to save a document	сохранять – сохранить документ (m.)
to open a file	открывать – открыть файл (m.)
to close a file	закрывать – закрыть файл
to attach a file	вкладывать – вложить, присоединять - присоединить файл

LESSON 33

A. More Verbs of Motion

Ходи́ть из одно́й ко́мнаты в другу́ю.	Walk from one room to another.
Е́здить из го́рода в го́род.	Travel from city to city.
Он хо́дит в библиоте́ку о́чень ча́сто.	He goes [walks] to the library very often.
Сего́дня мы идём в теа́тр.	Today we are going to the theatre.
Я всегда́ беру́ с собо́й бино́кль; я о́чень близору́кая.	I always take my glasses with me; I'm very nearsighted.
Мне не ну́жен бино́кль. Я дально-зо́ркий.	I don't need glasses. I'm farsighted.
Он взял кни́гу и ушёл.	He took the book and left.
Мой друг прие́хал вчера́ в Петербу́рг.	My friend arrived in Petersburg yesterday.
Он е́здит туда́ ка́ждое ле́то.	He goes there every summer.
Я уезжа́ю за́втра.	I'm leaving tomorrow.
Я уе́ду за́втра.	I'll leave tomorrow.
Я прие́ду во Владивосто́к то́лько че́рез во́семь дней.	I'll get to [arrive in] Vladivostok in only eight days.
Ско́лько вре́мени вы там бу́дете?	How long [how much time] will you be there?
Я ду́маю, что пробу́ду там то́лько о́коло двух неде́ль.	I think that I'll spend about two weeks there.

Я уже́ был оди́н раз во Владивосто́ке, но то́лько прое́здом по доро́ге в Аме́рику.	I've already been in Vladivostok once, but only [when] passing through on the way to America.
Я прилете́л из Сан-Франци́ско.	I flew from San Francisco.
Я хоте́ла бы пое́хать в Калифо́рнию.	I would like to go to California.
Говоря́т, что там замеча́тельная приро́да.	They say that the scenery [nature] there is magnificent.
Почему́ же вы не е́дете?	Well, why don't you go?
У меня́ о́чень ма́ло свобо́дного вре́мени.	I have very little free time.
Вы мо́жете вы́ехать в нача́ле ма́я и провести́ там весь ию́нь.	You can leave at the beginning of May and spend all of June there.
Но я до́лжен прие́хать обра́тно в Росси́ю в конце́ ию́ня.	But I have to be back in Russia by the end of June.
Не бо́йтесь, вы успе́ете.	Don't worry, you'll make it.
На самолёте мо́жно долете́ть о́чень бы́стро.	You can travel by plane very quickly.
Мо́жет быть, вы пра́вы. Попыта́юсь так и сде́лать.	Perhaps you're right. I'll try to do just that.

QUIZ 23

1. Бу́дьте как до́ма.	a. He goes there every summer.
2. Сего́дня мы идём в теа́тр.	b. Everything will be forgotten.
3. Он взял кни́гу и ушёл.	c. Where can I make a phone call?
4. Он е́здит туда́ ка́ждое ле́то.	d. Easier said than done.
5. Ско́лько вре́мени вы бу́дете там?	e. I'll try to do just that.
6. Всё бу́дет забы́то.	f. You can leave at the beginning of May.
7. У меня́ о́чень ма́ло свобо́дного вре́мени.	g. Make yourself at home.
8. Я был там по доро́ге домо́й.	h. Don't worry; you'll make it [you'll have time].
9. Говоря́т, что там замеча́тельная приро́да.	i. He has to be back in town by the end of June.
10. Отку́да мо́жно позвони́ть?	j. He took the book and left.
11. Соверше́нно ве́рно.	k. Today we are going to the theatre.
12. Ле́гче сказа́ть, чем сде́лать.	l. How long will you be there?
13. Мо́жет быть, вы пра́вы.	m. I have very little free time.
14. Попыта́юсь так и сде́лать.	n. She always takes her sister with her.
15. Он до́лжен прие́хать обра́тно в го́род в конце́ ию́ня.	o. Leave me alone.
16. Вы мо́жете вы́ехать в нача́ле ма́я.	p. May I speak with Vadim?
17. Не бо́йтесь, вы успе́ете.	q. Perhaps you're right.
18. Она́ всегда́ берёт с собо́й свою́ сестру́.	r. Quite right.
19. Мо́жно поговори́ть с Вади́мом?	s. They say that the scenery [nature] there is magnificent.
20. Оста́вьте меня́ в поко́е.	t. I passed by [was] there on my way home.

ANSWERS

1—g; 2—k; 3—j; 4—a; 5—l; 6—b; 7—m; 8—t; 9—s; 10—c; 11—r; 12—d; 13—q; 14—e; 15—i; 16—f; 17—h; 18—n; 19—p; 20—o.

LESSON 34

A. Newspapers, Books, Radio, and Television

Я хочу́ купи́ть газе́ту.	I want to buy a newspaper.
Я хочу́ купи́ть журна́л.	I want to buy a magazine.
У вас есть кни́ги на англи́йском языке́?	Do you have any books in English?
Есть музыка́льная програ́мма?	Is there a music station?
Есть програ́мма новосте́й?	Is there a news station?
Есть програ́мма прогно́за пого́ды?	Is there a weather station?
Во ско́лько нача́ло переда́чи?	What time is the program?
У вас есть телевизио́нная програ́мма?	Do you have a television guide?
Во ско́лько прогно́з пого́ды?	When is the weather forecast?
По како́му кана́лу идёт переда́ча?	What channel is the program on?

SUPPLEMENTAL VOCABULARY 13: ENTERTAINMENT

movie/film	фильм (m.), кино́ (n.) (coll.)
to go to the movies	ходи́ть – пойти́ в кино́
to see a movie	смотре́ть – посмотре́ть фильм (m.)

theater	театр (m.)
to see a play	посмотреть спектакль (m.)
opera	опера (f.)
concert	концерт (m.), на концерте
club	клуб (m.)
circus	цирк (m.)
ticket	билет (m.)
museum	музей (m.), музеи (nom., pl.)
gallery	галерея (f.)
painting	живопись (f.) (sg.)
sculpture	скульптура (f.)
television program	телевизионная программа (f.)
to watch television	смотреть – посмотреть телевизор (m.)
comedy	комедия (f.)
documentary	документальный фильм (m.)
drama	художественный фильм (m.)
book	книга (f.)
magazine	журнал (m.)
to read a book	читать – прочитать книгу
to read a magazine	читать – прочитать журнал
to listen to music	слушать – послушать музыку
song	песня (f.)
band	группа (f.)
the news	новости (pl.)
talk show	ток-шоу (n.)

to flip channels	переключать – переключить каналы
to have fun	получать – получить удовольствие (n.)
to be bored	скучать (imperf.)
funny	забавный, смешной
interesting	интересный
exciting	волнующий
scary	страшный
party	вечеринка (f.)
restaurant	ресторан (m.), кафе (n.)
to go to a party	ходить – пойти на вечеринку
to have a party	устраивать – устроить вечеринку
to dance	танцевать – потанцевать

B. AT THE POST OFFICE

Я ищу́ Главпочта́мт.	I'm looking for the main post office.
Где нахо́дится ближа́йший почто́вый я́щик?	Where's the nearest mailbox?
Ско́лько сто́ит отпра́вить письмо́ в Соединенные Шта́ты Аме́рики?	How much is it for a letter to the U.S.?
откры́тка	postcard
Я хочу́ купи́ть ма́рки.	I want to buy stamps.
Я хочу́ посла́ть э́ту посы́лку в Соединенные Шта́ты Аме́рики.	I want to send this package to the United States.

Мо́жно посла́ть телегра́мму в Нью-Йо́рк?	Can I send a telegram to New York?
Ско́лько сто́ит одна́ бу́ква?	How much is it per letter?
Придёт ли она́ за́втра у́тром?	Will it arrive tomorrow morning?
Како́е окно́ для телегра́мм?	Which window is it for telegrams?

C. MEETING AN OLD FRIEND

Я е́хал на по́езде в Москву́. По доро́ге мы останови́лись в Но́вгороде. Но́вгород не о́чень большо́й го́род, но тут есть прекра́сный вокза́л и о́чень хоро́ший рестора́н. По́езд стои́т там це́лый час. Я вы́шел из по́езда и пошёл погуля́ть по платфо́рме, а пото́м реши́л пойти́ в рестора́н пое́сть. Как то́лько я вошёл в рестора́н, я встре́тил мою́ знако́мую из Москвы́.

I was on my way to Moscow. On the way, we stopped in Novgorod. Novgorod is not a very large city, but there is a wonderful station there and a very good restaurant. The train was to be there for a whole hour. I got off the train and went for a stroll on the platform, and then I decided to go to the restaurant to eat. As soon as I walked into the restaurant, I ran into my friend from Moscow.

Серге́й:	*Sergei:*
Ве́ра Петро́вна, здра́вствуйте! Како́е интере́сное совпаде́ние!	Hello, Vera Petrovna! What an interesting coincidence.

Вéра:
**А! Сергéй Николáевич!
Как я рáда вас вúдеть!**

Vera:
Ah, Sergei
Nicholaevich! How
glad I am to see you!

Сергéй:
**Что вы здесь дéлаете?
Кудá вы éдете?**

Sergei:
What are you doing
here? Where are you
going?

Вéра:
**Я éду в Лáтвию.
У меня́ óтпуск.**

Vera:
I'm going to Latvia.
I'm on vacation.

Сергéй:
**Вы полýчите большóе
удовóльствие.**

Sergei:
You'll enjoy yourself
greatly [receive great
pleasure].

**Лáтвия прекрáсная
странá.**

Latvia is a magnificent
country.

Вéра:
**Да, я знáю. Я так
мнóго слы́шала и
так мнóго читáла о
мóре и соснóвых
лесáх. Я прóсто не
могý дождáться
той минýты, когдá
пéредо мнóй бýдет
мóре.**

Vera:
Yes, I know. I've
heard so much and
read so much about
the sea and pine
forests. I simply
can't wait for the
moment when I'll
see the sea
before me.

Сергéй:
**Ну, тепéрь ужé не
дóлго ждать. От
Нóвгорода óчень
блúзко. Давнó вы
из Москвы́?**

Sergei:
Well, now you won't
have to wait long.
It's very close to
Novgorod. Are you
away from Moscow
very long?

Вера:
**Нет, то́лько три дня.
Я вы́ехала в суббо́ту
у́тром.**

Сергей:
**Вы ви́дели моего́
бра́та пе́ред отъе́здом?**

Вера:
**Да, коне́чно, я зашла́
к нему́ в четве́рг
ве́чером, но его́ не́
бы́ло до́ма.**

Сергей:
**Зна́чит, вы его́ не
ви́дели?**

Вера:
**Нет, почему́ же? Я
оста́вила ему́ запи́ску,
и он позвони́л мне на
сле́дующий день и
пото́м пришёл ко мне.**

Сергей:
**Как там в Москве́?
Всё в поря́дке?**

Вера:
**Всё норма́льно. Жена́
ва́шего бра́та была́
больна́, но она́ уже́
попра́вилась и
чу́вствует себя́ непло́хо.**

Сергей:
**Да, я зна́ю. Брат мне
писа́л, и я о́чень
волнова́лся.**

Vera:
No, only three days.
I left Saturday
morning.

Sergei:
Did you see my brother
before leaving?

Vera:
Yes, of course, I
dropped in on him
Thursday evening,
but he wasn't home.

Sergei:
So [that means] you
didn't see him?

Vera:
No, why? I left him
a note, and he called
me the next day and
then came to see me.

Sergei:
How's everything in
Moscow? Everything
all right?

Vera:
Everything's fine.
Your brother's wife
was sick, but she has
recovered and feels
quite well.

Sergei:
Yes, I know. My brother
wrote me, and I was
very worried.

Вéра:
**Когда́ вы прие́дете в
    Москву́, пожа́луйста,
    позвони́те ма́ме и
    скажи́те, что встре́тили
    меня́. Вот она́
    удиви́тся! Серге́й
    Никола́евич, а
    вы уже́ обе́дали?**

Vera:
When you arrive in
    Moscow, please call
    my mother and say
    that you ran into me.
    She'll be so sur-
    prised. Sergei
    Nicholaevich,
    have you already
    eaten?

Серге́й:
**Нет, коне́чно нет,
    пойдёмте вме́сте и
    перекýсим.**

Sergei:
No, of course not.
    Let's go and
    have a bite together.

Вéра:
**Вот хорошо́, а то я
    про́сто умира́ю с
    го́лоду.**

Vera:
That's good, I'm sim-
    ply dying of hunger.

Серге́й:
**Вот здесь свобо́дный
    сто́лик. Дава́йте ся́дем
    здесь. Когда́ вы
    бýдете в Ри́ге, не
    забýдьте подня́ться
    на Пороховýю Ба́шню.**

Sergei:
Here's an empty
    table. Let's sit here.
    When you're in Riga,
    don't forget to go up
    to the top of the
    fortress tower.

Вéра:
**Говоря́т, что э́то о́чень
    интере́сно. Э́то о́чень
    ста́рое зда́ние, пра́вда?**

Vera:
They say that it's
    very interesting.
    It is a very old
    building, right?

Серге́й:
**Соверше́нно ве́рно. И
    вы зна́ете, оттýда
    открыва́ется
    изуми́тельный вид на
    весь го́род.**

Sergei:
Quite right. And you
    know, from there,
    there is [opens up]
    an amazing view of
    the whole city.

Вéра:
**Мне дáже не вéрится,
что я всё э́то увѝжу.**

Vera:
I can hardly believe
[even don't believe]
that I will see all
this.

**За обéдом я рассказáл Вéре Петрóвне всё,
что я знал о Лáтвии: кудá лýчше всегó пойтѝ,
что посмотрéть, где мóжно хорошó поéсть. Час
прошёл óчень бы́стро, и я чуть не опоздáл на
свой пóезд.**

At dinner I told Vera Petrovna all that I knew about
Latvia: the best places to go, what to see, and the good
places to eat. The hour passed very quickly, and I was
almost late for my train.

LESSON 35

A. END OF THE VACATION

**Как бы́стро летѝт
врéмя!**

How quickly time
flies.

**Вот ужé четы́ре недéли
с тех пор, как я на-
чалá путешéствовать.**

[Here] it's four weeks
already since I
started to travel.

**К сожалéнию, мой
óтпуск подхóдит к
концý.**

Unfortunately my
vacation is coming
to an end.

**Мне нýжно соби-
рáться.**

I have to start pack-
ing.

У меня́ три чемодáна.   I have three suitcases.

Оди́н о́чень большо́й и два други́х поме́ньше.	One is very big, and the other two somewhat smaller.
В большо́й чемода́н помеща́ется о́чень мно́го веще́й.	A great many things can be put into the big suitcase.
Но зато́ его́ о́чень тяжело́ нести́.	But on the other hand, it's very heavy to carry.
К сча́стью, мой друг пое́дет со мно́й на вокза́л.	Luckily, my friend will go to the station with me.
Он о́чень си́льный.	He's very strong.
Ему́ всё легко́.	Everything is light for him.
Ну́жно бу́дет купи́ть биле́ты зара́нее, что́бы не стоя́ть в о́череди.	I'll have to buy tickets beforehand in order not to stand in line.
Ну́жно не забы́ть позвони́ть всем знако́мым.	I [one] must not forget to telephone all my friends.
Ну́жно бу́дет попроща́ться со все́ми.	I'll have to say goodbye to [take leave of] all of them.
Я сде́лала о́чень мно́го сни́мков и отдала́ их прояви́ть.	I took many pictures and left [gave] them to be developed.
Наде́юсь, что все фотогра́фии бу́дут гото́вы до моего́ отъе́зда.	I hope that all the pictures will be ready before my departure.
Я ещё не получи́ла бельё из сти́рки. Оно́ должно́ быть уже́ гото́во.	I still haven't gotten back my laundry. It should be ready by now.

Ну, вот ве́щи уже́ уло́жены.	Well, my things are all packed.
За́втра мы е́дем домо́й. Коне́ц о́тпуску. До сле́дующего го́да.	Tomorrow we are going home. End of my vacation. Until next year.
В бу́дущем году́ мы опя́ть собира́емся пое́хать куда́-нибудь.	We are planning to go somewhere again next year.
Мне о́чень хо́чется пое́хать в Сре́днюю А́зию.	I'd very much like to go to Central Asia.
Говоря́т, что там о́чень интере́сно.	They say [it is said] that it's very interesting there.
Там мно́го стари́нных городо́в.	There are many old cities there.
Наприме́р, го́род Ташке́нт де́лится на ста́рый го́род и но́вый го́род. Э́тот го́род изве́стен уже́ с седьмо́го ве́ка.	For instance, the city Tashkent is divided into the Old City and the New City. This city dates back to [is known from] the seventh century.
Там есть па́мятники дре́вней архитекту́ры пятна́дцатого и шестна́дцатого веко́в.	There are relics of ancient architecture of the fifteenth and sixteenth centuries.

QUIZ 24

1. Я про́сто не могу́ дожда́ться той мину́ты, когда́ пе́редо мной бу́дет мо́ре.

   a. They say that it's very interesting.

2. В э́том го́роде есть прекра́сный вокза́л и о́чень хоро́ший рестора́н.

   b. From there, there is [opens up] an amazing view of the whole city.

3. Како́е интере́сное
   совпаде́ние!

4. Когда́ я вошёл в рестора́н,
   я встре́тил мою́ знако́мую.

5. Вот свобо́дный сто́лик.

6. Говоря́т, что э́то о́чень
   интере́сно.

7. Дава́йте ся́дем здесь.

8. Отту́да открыва́ется
   изуми́тельный вид на
   весь го́род.

9. По́езд стои́т здесь це́лый
   час.

10. Мне да́же не ве́рится,
    что я всё э́то уви́жу.

11. Пожа́луйста, позвони́те
    мое́й сестре́ и скажи́те,
    что вы встре́тили меня́.

12. Я чуть не опозда́л на
    свой по́езд.

13. Как бы́стро лети́т вре́мя!

14. Я хочу́ купи́ть газе́ту.

15. К сча́стью, мой друг
    пое́дет со мной на
    вокза́л.

16. Ну́жно не забы́ть
    позвони́ть всем знако́мым.

17. Ско́лько сто́ит отпра́вить
    письмо́?

18. В бу́дущем году́ мы опя́ть
    пое́дем куда́-нибудь.

19. Говоря́т, что там о́чень
    интере́сно.

20. Э́тот го́род изве́стен
    уже́ с седьмо́го ве́ка.

c. I was almost late for my
   train.

d. The train stops here for a
   whole hour.

e. I want to buy a newspaper.

f. I must not forget to tele-
   phone all my friends.

g. Please call my sister and
   tell her that you met me.

h. How quickly time flies!

i. Luckily, my friend will
   go to the station with me.

j. How much is it for a
   letter?

k. They say that it's very
   interesting there.

l. Next year we will
   go somewhere again.

m. This city dates back to [is
   known from] the seventh
   century.

n. Let's sit here.

o. What an interesting
   coincidence!

p. Here's an empty table.

q. I simply can't wait for the
   moment when I'll see the
   sea before [in front of] me.

r. I can hardly believe that
   I will see all this.

s. In this city there is a
   wonderful station and a
   very good restaurant.

t. When I walked into the
   restaurant, I met my
   friend.

ANSWERS

1—q; 2—s; 3—o; 4—t; 5—p; 6—a; 7—n; 8—b; 9—d; 10—r; 11—g;
12—c; 13—h; 14—e; 15—i; 16—f; 17—j; 18—l; 19—k; 20—m.

SUPPLEMENTAL VOCABULARY 14: SPORTS
AND RECREATION

soccer/football	футбол (m.)
basketball	баскетбол (m.)
baseball	бейсбол (m.)
american football	американский футбол
hockey	хоккей (m.)
tennis	теннис (m.)
gymnastics	гимнастика (f.)
figure skating	фигурное катание (n.)
swimming	плавание (n.)
volleyball	волейбол (m.)
running	бег (m.)
jogging	бег трусцой
game	игра (f.)
team	команда (f.)
stadium	стадион (m.)
coach	тренер (m.)
player	игрок (m.)
champion	чемпион (m.)
ball	мяч (m.)
(to go) hiking	ходить пешком, ходить в поход
(to go) camping	ходить (в поход) с палаткой
to play (a sport)	заниматься (imper.) спортом
to play (a game)	играть - сыграть игру
to win	выигрывать - выиграть
to lose	проигрывать - проиграть

to draw/tie	играть - сыграть вничью/ничья (f.)
cards	карты (pl.)
pool/billiards	пул (m.)/бильярд (m.)
chess	шахматы (pl.)
checkers	шашки (pl.)
backgammon	нарды (pl.)
bingo	лото (n.)
crossword puzzle	кроссворд (m.)

LESSON 36

A. MAY OR CAN

The words "may" and "may not," and "can" and "cannot" are expressed in Russian by мо́жно (it is possible) and нельзя́ (it is not possible).

Мо́жно вы́йти?	May I go out?
Нет, нельзя́.	No, you may not.

Нельзя́ is a Russian word for which there is no exact English equivalent.

Нельзя́ сказа́ть, что здесь жа́рко.	You would not say that it is hot here.
Здесь нельзя́ кури́ть.	You (one) cannot (may not) smoke here.

Мо́жно?	Нельзя́
May I?	No, you may not.
Can I?	No, you cannot.
Is it possible?	It is impossible.
Is it allowed?	It is not allowed.

Мóжно and нельзя́ are adverbs and therefore do
not change their form.

B.   May I?

Cáша:	*Sasha:*
Здесь мóжно кури́ть?	May one smoke here?
Мúша:	*Misha:*
Нет, здесь нельзя́ кури́ть. Посмотри́те, вот там напи́сано: «Кури́ть воспреща́ется».	No, (there's) no smoking here. Look, the sign says [it's written there]: "Smoking forbidden."
Cáша:	*Sasha:*
А где вообще́ мóжно кури́ть?	Where can one smoke?
Мúша:	*Misha:*
В теа́трах мóжно кури́ть в кури́тельной кóмнате/кури́лке (coll.) и́ли на у́лице. В поезда́х В та́мбуре.	In theatres one may smoke in the smoking room or outside. In trains [one can smoke] by the doors.
Cáша:	*Sasha:*
У меня́ нет спи́чек. Да́йте мне, пожа́луйста, спи́чки. Рýсские сигаре́ты совсе́м не таки́е, как америка́нские. К ним на́до привы́кнуть.	I have no matches. Please give me matches. Russian cigarettes are not at all like American (cigarettes). One must get used to them.
Мúша:	*Misha:*
Куре́ние вообще́ о́чень плоха́я привы́чка.	Smoking is, in general, a very bad habit.

Са́ша:
**Соверше́нно с ва́ми
согла́сен, но я о́чень
люблю́ кури́ть.**

Sasha:
I completely agree
with you, but I love
to smoke.

Ми́ша:
**Вы уже́ вы́курили всю
па́чку. Хва́тит на
сего́дня.**

Misha:
You've already fin-
ished a whole pack.
Enough for today.

Са́ша:
**Ничего́ подо́бного. Я
вы́курил то́лько
полпа́чки.**

Sasha:
Nothing of the sort.
I smoked only half a
pack.

Ми́ша:
**Пе́йте бо́льше молока́.
Э́то вам о́чень
поле́зно.**

Misha:
Drink more milk. It's
very good for you.

Са́ша:
**Я не люблю́ пить и
есть то, что поле́зно.**

Sasha:
I don't like to drink
and eat the things
that are good for me.

Ми́ша:
**Вы что хоти́те, то и
де́лаете!**

Misha:
You do whatever
you want!

Са́ша:
**Коне́чно! Что хочу́, то
и де́лаю.**

Sasha:
Of course! What I
want (to do), I do.

Ми́ша:
**Кури́ть мно́го–вре́дно,
а пить мно́го молока́
поле́зно.**

Misha:
Smoking a lot is
harmful, but drink-
ing a lot of milk is
good for you.

Са́ша:
**Мо́жет бы́ть, э́то и так,
но я не люблю́ молоко́.**

Sasha:
Maybe that's so, but
I don't like milk.

Ми́ша: *Misha:*
Все де́ти выраста́ют на   All children grow up
  молоке́.   on milk.
Са́ша: *Sasha:*
Когда́ я был ребёнком,   When I was a baby I
  я пил молоко́, а тепе́рь   drank milk, and now
  я курю́.   I smoke.
Ми́ша: *Misha:*
Вы свобо́дный челове́к.   You're a free person.
  Де́лайте, что хоти́те.   Do as you please.

C. I CAN'T

Мне нельзя́ выходи́ть.   I can't go out. I
  Я простуди́лся. У меня́   caught a cold. I have
  боли́т го́рло и голова́.   a sore throat and a
                                    headache.

У вас на́сморк. Вам   You have a head
  ну́жно лежа́ть в   cold. You have to
  посте́ли. До́ктор   stay in bed. The doc-
  сказа́л, что вам   tor said that you
  нельзя́ кури́ть.   can't smoke.

На э́тот конце́рт   It's impossible to get
  нельзя́ попа́сть: все   to that concert. All
  биле́ты про́даны.   the tickets have been
                                   sold.

О́чень жа́ль, что   Too bad that we
  нельзя́. Пойдём   can't go. Let's go
  куда́-нибудь в друго́е   somewhere else.
  ме́сто.

Ему́ нельзя́ ходи́ть   He can't take the
  по ле́стнице. У него́   stairs. He has a weak
  сла́бое се́рдце.   heart.

Он живёт как нельзя́   He can't live any
  лу́чше.   better than he does.

Где ваш друг Николай сегодня?	Where is your friend Nicholas today?
Я никогда не знаю, где он.	I never know where he is [could be].

QUIZ 25

1. Вы что хотите, то и делаете.
2. Курить много вредно, а пить много молока полезно.
3. Нельзя сказать, что это всегда так.
4. На этот концерт нельзя попасть: все билеты проданы.
5. Ему нельзя ходить по лестнице. У него слабое сердце.
6. Он живёт, как нельзя лучше.
7. От кого вы получили письмо?
8. С кем вы были в театре вчера?
9. Что значит это слово?
10. Чего только нет в этом магазине!
11. Не понимаю—о чём тут говорить?
12. Как вы себя чувствуете?
13. У них есть всё, что вам нужно.
14. Мне хочется пить.
15. Я могу сказать только несколько слов по-русски.

a. They have everything you need.
b. What does this word mean?
c. I can say only a few words in Russian.
d. What they don't have in this store!
e. You pronounce Russian words badly.
f. I don't understand—what is there to talk about?
g. I'm thirsty.
h. What kind of wine do you want—white or red?
i. Excuse me, but I don't understand you.
j. Where are you going to have dinner after work?
k. You do whatever you want.
l. It's difficult for me to understand when you speak so fast.
m. He can't live any better than he does.
n. With whom were you in the theatre yesterday?
o. Smoking a lot is harmful, but drinking a lot of milk is good for you.

16. Вы пло́хо произно́сите
    ру́сские слова́.

p. From whom did you get
   a letter?

17. Мне тру́дно понима́ть,
    когда́ вы говори́те так
    бы́стро.

q. It's impossible to get to
   that concert. All the tickets have been sold.

18. Прости́те, но я не
    понима́ю вас.

r. He can't take the stairs.
   He has a weak heart.

19. Како́е вино́ вы хоти́те—
    бе́лое и́ли кра́сное?

s. How are you feeling?

20. Куда́ вы идёте у́жинать
    по́сле рабо́ты?

t. You [one] can't say that
   it is always so.

ANSWERS

1—k; 2—o; 3—t; 4—q; 5—r; 6—m; 7—p; 8—n; 9—b; 10—d;
11—f; 12—s; 13—a; 14—g; 15—c; 16—e; 17—l; 18—i; 19—h;
20—j.

LESSON 37

A. LOST AND FOUND

Мы не зна́ли доро́ги и
потеря́ли мно́го
вре́мени по доро́ге
в музе́й.

We didn't know the
way and lost a lot of
time on the way to
the museum.

Он потеря́л свой
бума́жник.

He lost his wallet.

Об э́том ну́жно сказа́ть
милиционе́ру и́ли
заяви́ть пря́мо в
мили́цию.

You must report that
to a policeman or go
directly to the police
station.

Е́сли кто́-нибудь найдёт
э́тот бума́жник, то его́,
по всей вероя́тности,
верну́т.

If someone finds
this wallet, he will,
in all probability,
return it.

Она́ ничего́ никогда́ не теря́ет.	She never loses anything.
Вчера́ она́ потеря́ла одну́ перча́тку.	Yesterday she lost one glove.
Кто́-то её нашёл.	Someone found it.
Она́ лежи́т тепе́рь на столе́ у администра́тора гости́ницы.	It's now at the hotel manager's desk.
Когда́ я хожу́ пешко́м по у́лице, я всегда́ что́-нибудь нахожу́.	When I walk along the street, I always find something.
Сего́дня я нашёл о́чень хоро́шую перьеву́ю ру́чку.	Today I found a very good fountain pen.
Мне так жаль того́, кто её потеря́л.	I'm so sorry for the person who lost it.
Что вы и́щете?	What are you looking for?
Я всегда́ что́-нибудь ищу́.	I'm always looking for something.
Ищи́те–и вы найдёте.	Seek, and you will find.
В Москве́ не тру́дно найти́ хоро́ший теа́тр.	In Moscow it's not difficult to find a good theatre.
Я потеря́лся и не знал, куда́ идти́.	I lost my way and didn't know where to go.
Я растеря́лся и не знал, что сказа́ть.	I became flustered and didn't know what to say.
Я заблуди́лся и не мог найти́ доро́ги.	I got lost and couldn't find the way.
В э́том го́роде о́чень не тру́дно заблуди́ться.	It's not hard to lose one's way in this city.

Э́то о́чень ста́рый
го́род. У́лицы у́зкие
икраси́вые, и никогда́
не изве́стно, куда́
у́лица повернёт и
куда́ она́ вас
приведёт.

This is a very old
city. The streets are
narrow and beautiful,
and you never know
where the street turns
and where it will
lead you.

Ма́ленькие у́зкие
у́лицы называ́ются
по-ру́сски переу́лками.

Little narrow streets
are called "pereulok"
in Russian.

В го́роде, где я
когда́-то жил, была́
у́лица, кото́рая
называ́лась
«Театра́льный пере-
у́лок».

In the city where
I lived one time,
there was a street
that was called
"Theatre Pereulok"
[Theatre Lane].

Е́сли переу́лок не
проходно́й, то он
называ́ется тупико́м.

If a "pereulok" has a
dead end, it is called
a "tupik."

О́чень ча́сто говоря́т:
«Я попа́л в тупи́к».
Э́то зна́чит, что вы в
тако́м положе́нии, из
кото́рого нет вы́хода.
Наде́юсь, что никто́
из нас никогда́ не
попадёт в тупи́к.

Very often it is said:
"I got into a tupik."
This means that you
are in the kind of
situation that has no
way out. I hope that
not one of us ever
falls into a tupik.

Из ка́ждого тупика́
мо́жно вы́йти тем же
путём, каки́м вы в
него́ пришли́.

It is possible to get out
of every tupik by the
same road through
which you entered.

Иногда́ ну́жно
сде́лать шаг наза́д.
Все мы де́лаем иногда́
оши́бки.

Sometimes it is neces-
sary to take a step
backward. We all
make mistakes some-
times.

Не ошибáется тóлько тот, кто ничегó не дéлает.	Only he who does nothing makes no mistakes.
Я ошúбся и пошёл напрáво, а нáдо бы́ло идтú налéво.	I made a mistake and turned to the right, and I should have gone to the left.
Óчень трýдно говорúть без ошúбок.	It's very difficult to speak without mistakes.
Óчень трýдно писáть без ошúбок.	It's very difficult to write without mistakes.
Легкó дéлать тóлько то, что вы хорошó знáете.	It's only easy to do that which you know well.
Рабóтайте, занимáйтесь, слýшайте, повторя́йте, читáйте, запоминáйте.	Work, study, listen, repeat, read, memorize.
Вы́учите всё, что на э́тих дúсках, и вы бýдете говорúть по-рýсски.	Learn everything that is on these CDs, and you will speak Russian.

B. THE IMPERATIVE MOOD

The imperative of a verb is formed from the second-person singular present tense. For the singular imperative, replace the ending with -й if the ending is a vowel, with -и if the ending is a consonant (and the first-person singular form of the verb is stressed on the ending), and with -ь if the ending is a consonant (but the first-person singular form is not stressed on the ending). If the ending has two consonants, add an -и regardless of the stress. For the plural imperative, add -те to the singular.

Infinitive	Second-Pers. Singular	Familiar, Singular	Plural, Polite
писа́ть to write	пи́ш-ешь	пиши́!	пиши́те!
повторя́ть to repeat	повторя́-ешь	повторя́й!	повторя́йте!
броса́ть to throw	броса́-ешь	броса́й!	броса́йте!
рабо́тать to work	рабо́та-ешь	рабо́тай!	рабо́тайте!
чита́ть to read	чита́-ешь	чита́й!	чита́йте!
по́мнить to remember	по́мн-ишь	по́мни!	по́мните!

The reflexive verb retains its endings: -ся after a consonant or after -й, and -сь after a vowel.

мы́ться to wash (oneself)	мо́-ешься	мо́йся!	мо́йтесь!
занима́ться to study	занима́-ешься	занима́йся!	занима́йтесь!

In giving an order indirectly to a third person, the forms пусть and пуска́й (coll.) are used with the third-person singular of the verb:

Пусть он чита́ет.	Let him read.	[He should read.]
Пуска́й она́ говори́т.	Let her speak.	[She should speak.]

C. Even More on Perfective and Imperfective Verbs

This lesson again shows the use of perfective and imperfective verbs:

IMPERFECTIVE	PERFECTIVE
теря́ть	потеря́ть
находи́ть	найти́

Он потеря́л свой бума́жник.	He lost his wallet (once, this time: perfective).
Она́ ничего́ никогда́ не теря́ет.	She never loses anything (at any time: imperfective).
Я всегда́ что́-нибудь нахожу́.	I always find things (all the time: imperfective).
Сего́дня я нашёл . . .	Today I found (one time, one action: perfective) . . .

D. Word Study

голова́	head
ва́жный	important
вопро́с	question, issue
по́здно	late
де́ло	matter, business
коне́чно	of course
за́втра	tomorrow
ско́ро	soon
да́льше	further

QUIZ 26

1. Я никуда́ не иду́ по́сле обе́да.
2. Чья газе́та там на столе́?
3. Когда́ я хожу́ пешко́м по у́лице, я всегда́ что́-нибудь нахожу́.
4. Как называ́ется э́тот го́род?
5. Я растеря́лся и не знал, что сказа́ть.
6. Как вам не сты́дно, так ско́ро забы́ть меня́!

a. You may be right.
b. All the best, and have a pleasant trip.
c. It's very easy to lose one's way in this city.
d. It is possible to get out of every blind alley by the same road through which you entered.
e. Tupik is a situation that has no way out.
f. When I came here, I had two hundred thousand rubles.

7. Сегодня я нашёл очень хорошую перьевую ручку.

g. I am so sorry for the person who lost it.

8. Как я рад, что встретил вас!

h. I lost my way and didn't know where to go.

9. Это как раз то, что мне надо.

i. Aren't you ashamed to have forgotten me so soon!

10. Это гораздо труднее, чем вы думаете.

j. I became flustered and didn't know what to say.

11. Возможно, что вы правы.

k. Whose newspaper is on the table?

12. Мне так жаль того, кто её потерял.

l. How glad I am that I met you!

13. Мне нужно идти. Мой поезд скоро отходит.

m. I am not going anywhere after dinner.

14. Всего хорошего и счастливого пути.

n. Today I found a very good fountain pen.

15. Я потерялся и не знал, куда идти.

o. It's just the thing I need.

16. В этом городе очень легко заблудиться.

p. Only he who does nothing makes no mistakes.

17. Из каждого тупика можно выйти тем же путём, каким вы в него вошли.

q. What is the name of this city?

18. Тупик–это положение, из которого нет выхода.

r. It's far more difficult than you think.

19. Когда я приехал сюда, у меня было двести тысяч рублей.

s. I have to go. My train is leaving soon.

20. Не ошибается только тот, кто ничего не делает.

t. When I walk along the street, I always find something.

ANSWERS

1—m; 2—k; 3—t; 4—q; 5—j; 6—i; 7—n; 8—l; 9—o; 10—r; 11—a; 12—g; 13—s; 14—b; 15—h; 16—c; 17—d; 18—e; 19—f; 20—p.

LESSON 38

A. Buying Gifts

Ольга:

Я сего́дня иду́ в магази́н. Мне ну́жно ко́е-что́ купи́ть. Хоти́те пойти́ со мной?

Olga:

I'm going to the store today. I have to buy something. Do you want to go with me?

Игорь:

Мне что́-то не хо́чется, но я ду́маю, что всё же пойду́.

Igor:

I don't feel like it, but I think I'll go anyway.

В како́й магази́н вы хоти́те пойти́?

What store do you want to go to?

Ольга:

Я хочу́ пойти́ в магази́н, кото́рый называ́ется «Де́тский мир». Там есть всё для дете́й любо́го во́зраста.

Olga:

I want to go to a store called "Children's World." There they have everything for children of any age.

Игорь:

Ну, е́сли так, то я пойду́ с ва́ми.

Igor:

Oh, if that's so, then I'll go with you.

Ольга:

Вот и хорошо́. Мне ну́жно купи́ть ю́бку племя́ннице и каку́ю-нибудь игру́шку сы́ну.

Olga:

That's good. I have to buy a skirt for my niece and some sort of toy for my son.

Игорь:

Како́й большо́й магази́н! Как здесь интере́сно.

Igor:

What a big store! How interesting it is here.

Óльга:	*Olga:*
Пойдёмте на второй этáж. Там продаю́т ю́бки.	Let's go to the second floor. That's where skirts are sold.
Úгорь:	*Igor:*
Вот óчень краси́вая ю́бка. Вам нрáвится?	There's a very pretty skirt. Do you like it?
Óльга:	*Olga:*
Нет, не óчень. Мне не нрáвится э́тот цвет. Сли́шком я́ркий.	Not very much. I don't like that color. It's too bright.
Úгорь:	*Igor:*
Да что вы! Совсéм нет! Ведь вáша племя́нница такáя молодáя дéвушка.	Oh, what do you mean! No, it's not! [Not at all!] Why, your niece is still so young!
Óльга:	*Olga:*
Да, конéчно. Но онá óчень скрóмная и предпочитáет чтó-нибудь попрóще. Вот э́та сéрая ю́бка бу́дет лу́чше, прáвда?	Yes, of course. But she is very modest and prefers something simpler. Here, this gray skirt will be better, don't you think?
Úгорь:	*Igor:*
Совершéнно вéрно.	Quite right.
Óльга:	*Olga:*
Извини́те, скóлько стóит э́та ю́бка?	Excuse me, how much does this skirt cost?
Продавщи́ца:	*Salesperson:*
Пятьсóт пятьдеся́т рублéй. Э́то чи́стая шéрсть. И óчень хорошó нóсится.	Five hundred fifty rubles. It's pure wool. And it wears very well.
Óльга:	*Olga:*
Да? Я её возьму́. Я покупáю не для	Really? I'll take it. I'm not buying it for myself, so

себя, и если размер
не подойдёт, можно
будет поменять?

if the size isn't right,
may I exchange it?

Продавщица:

Конечно, в любое
время. Только не в
воскресенье. По
воскресеньям наш
магазин закрыт. Это
наш выходной день.

Salesperson:

Of course. At any time.
But not on a Sunday.
Our store is closed on
Sundays. That's our day
off.

Игорь:

А почему у них
выходной день в
воскресенье?

Igor:

But why do they have
their day off on
Sunday?

Ольга:

В России в
воскресенье
некоторые магазины
закрыты.

Olga:

In Russia some stores are
closed on Sunday.

Игорь:

Вы ещё ничего не
купили вашему сыну.

Igor:

You haven't bought any-
thing for your son yet.

Ольга:

Ах да! Вот очень
хороший
конструктор. Он
очень любит
строить. Сколько
стоят эти кубики?

Olga:

Oh, yes. Here are some
very nice blocks. He
loves to build. How
much are these blocks?

Продавщица:

Семьсот тридцать
рублей.

Salesperson:

Seven hundred thirty
rubles.

Ольга:

Это дорого, но я всё
же их возьму. Вот
тысяча триста

Olga:

That's a little expensive,
but I'll take them any-
way. Here are one

рубле́й.	thousand three hundred rubles.
Продавщи́ца:	*Salesperson:*
Не забу́дьте, пожа́луй-ста, ва́шу сда́чу.	Don't forget your change, please.
И́горь/О́льга:	*Igor/Olga:*
До свида́ния. Спаси́бо.	Good-bye. Thank you.

SUPPLEMENTAL VOCABULARY 15:
   CLOTHING

shirt	рубашка (f.)
pants	брюки (pl.), штаны (pl.) (coll.)
jeans	джинсы (pl.)
tee shirt	футболка (f.)
shoe(s)	туфля (f.) – туфли (pl.)
sock(s)	носок (m.) – носки (pl.)
belt	ремень (m.), ремни (nom., pl.)
sneakers/tennis shoes	кроссовки (pl.)/ теннисные туфли (pl.)
dress	платье (n.)
skirt	юбка (f.)
blouse	блузка (f.)
suit	костюм (m.)
hat	шляпа (f.)
glove(s)	перчатка (f.), перчатки (pl.)
scarf	шарф (m.)
jacket	пиджак (m.)
coat	пальто (n.) (indeclinable)
earring(s)	серьга (f.), серьги (nom., pl.)

bracelet	браслет (m.)
necklace	ожерелье (n.), ожерелья (nom., pl.)
eyeglasses	очки (pl.)
sunglasses	тёмные очки (pl.), солнцезащитные очки (pl.) (formal)
watch	часы (pl.)
ring	кольцо (n.)
underpants	трусы (pl.)
undershirt	майка (f.)
bathing trunks	плавки (pl.)
bathing suit	купальник (m.)
pyjamas	пижама (f.)
cotton	хлопок (m.)
leather	кожа (f.)
silk	шелк (m.)
size	размер (m.)
to wear	носить (imperf.)

B. USE OF THE PARTICLES To AND Нибудь

кто́-то	someone	кто́-нибудь	anyone
где́-то	somewhere	где́-нибудь	anywhere
что́-то	something	что́-нибудь	anything
куда́-то	somewhere	куда́-нибудь	anywhere
почему́-то	for some reason	почему́-нибудь	for any reason

To is used to show that something is known:

Кто́-то пришёл.

Someone came. (I don't know who, but someone did come.)

Он куда́-то пое́дет за́втра.

He is going somewhere tomorrow. (I don't know where, but he does, and it is definite that he is going.)

Нибудь is used to show that nothing is known:

Кто-нибудь придёт.

Somebody will come. (I don't know who it will be, I don't know if anyone will come, but I think that somebody will come.)

Мне хо́чется куда-нибудь пое́хать.

I feel like going somewhere. (I don't know where, and I don't know if I will, but I feel like it.)

QUIZ 27

1. Я встаю́ в во́семь часо́в утра́.
2. Э́тот биле́т сто́ит шестьсо́т рубле́й.
3. Вы ещё ничего́ не купи́ли ва́шему сы́ну.
4. Покажи́те мне, пожа́луйста, э́ту кни́гу.
5. Мне не нра́вится э́тот цвет. Сли́шком я́ркий.
6. Вот э́та се́рая ю́бка бу́дет лу́чше, пра́вда?
7. По воскресе́ньям наш магази́н закры́т.
8. Э́то до́рого, но я всё же их возьму́.
9. Не забу́дьте, пожа́луй-ста, ва́шу сда́чу.
10. Мне о́чень нра́вится э́тот го́род.
11. Я всегда́ пью ко́фе с молоко́м.
12. Э́то де́ло вку́са.
13. Како́е вку́сное пиро́жное!
14. Спекта́кль начина́ется без че́тверти во́семь.
15. Он ничего́ не хо́чет де́лать.

a. On Sundays our store is closed.
b. It's a question of taste.
c. He doesn't want to do anything.
d. He prefers something simpler.
e. The performance starts at a quarter of eight.
f. How often do the buses run?
g. What a delicious pastry!
h. I get up at eight o'clock in the morning.
i. She was in the store and didn't buy anything.
j. Every five minutes.
k. This ticket costs six hundred rubles.
l. You haven't bought anything for your son yet.
m. Do you know what is playing at the theatre today?
n. I don't like that color. It's too bright.
o. That's expensive, but I'll take them anyway.

16. Она́ была́ в магази́не
    и ничего́ не купи́ла.

p. I like this city very much.

17. Он предпочита́ет
    что́-нибудь попро́ще.

q. Here, this gray skirt will be
   better, don't you think [isn't
   it true]?

18. Как ча́сто хо́дят
    тролле́йбусы?

r. I always drink coffee with
   milk.

19. Ка́ждые пять мину́т.

s. Don't forget your change,
   please.

20. Вы не зна́ете, что
    сего́дня идёт в теа́тре?

t. Please, show me this book.

ANSWERS

1—h; 2—k; 3—l; 4—t; 5—n; 6—q; 7—a; 8—o; 9—s; 10—p; 11—
r; 12—b; 13—g; 14—e; 15—c; 16—i; 17—d; 18—f; 19—j; 20—m.

LESSON 39

A. Two Colleagues

Илья́:
**Здра́вствуйте, ми́лая
Наде́жда
Гео́ргиевна!**

Ilya:
Hello, dear Nadezhda
Georgievna!

Наде́жда:
**Здра́вствуйте, Илья́
Петро́вич! Как я
ра́да вас ви́деть! Я
как раз собира́лась
вам позвони́ть.**

Nadezhda:
How are you, Ilya
Petrovich! I am so
happy to see you. I was
just about to call you.

Илья́:
А что тако́е?

Ilya:
What's the matter?

Наде́жда:
**У меня́ в суббо́ту
бу́дет приём.**

Nadezhda:
I am having a reception
on Saturday. A group

Приезжа́ет гру́ппа коммерса́нтов из Росси́и. С не́которыми из них вы уже знако́мы по рабо́те в ба́нке. По́мните Васи́лия Смирно́ва и Никола́я Радзи́нского?

of businessmen from Russia is coming. Some of them you already know through your work at the bank. Do you remember Vasily Smirnov and Nikolai Radzinsky?

Илья́:

Ilya:

Да, да, коне́чно. Как я могу́ вам помо́чь?

Yes, yes, of course. How can I help you?

Наде́жда:

Nadezhda:

Да́же нело́вко проси́ть. Де́ло в том, что Джим, мой муж, заинтересо́ван в организа́ции совме́стного предприя́тия в Оде́ссе. Но нужна́ подде́ржка ме́стных власте́й. Тепе́рь, коне́чно, Украи́на незави́сима и поэ́тому всё осложнено́. Кро́ме того́, Джим о́чень пло́хо говори́т по-ру́сски. Коро́че, нужны́ перево́дчики. Я, коне́чно, сама́ бу́ду переводи́ть, но гру́ппа больша́я. В о́бщем, са́ми понима́ете.

It's awkward to even ask. The thing is that Jim, my husband, is interested in organizing a joint venture in Odessa. But the support of local authorities is what is needed. Now, of course, the Ukraine is independent, and everything is complicated. Besides, Jim's Russian is very bad. In short we need inter- preters. I will certainly interpret myself, but the group is large. Well, you understand.

Илья:

Наде́жда Гео́ргиевна! О чём речь! Вы же зна́ете, что я всегда́ гото́в помо́чь. Да, к тому́ же, я сам хоте́л переговори́ть с Радзи́нским насчёт капиталовложе́ний в ру́сские компа́нии.

Ilya:

Nadezhda Georgievna! What are you talking about! You know that I am always ready to help. Besides, I wanted to have a chat with Radzinsky myself about investments in Russian companies.

Наде́жда:

Ну и сла́ва Бо́гу! В о́бщем, жду́ вас у себя́ в 7 часо́в. Я заказа́ла пирожки́, икру́ и, коне́чно, я́щик шампа́нского и ру́сскую во́дку.

Nadezhda:

Thank God! So I am expecting you at my place at seven o'clock. I ordered meat pies, caviar, and, of course, a case of champagne and Russian vodka.

Илья:

Пока́ перевожу́, придётся без во́дки обойти́сь.

Ilya:

I will have to do without vodka while interpreting.

Наде́жда:

Коне́чно, коне́чно. Огро́мное спаси́бо. Жду.

Nadezhda:

Of course, of course. I am very grateful. I'm expecting you.

SUPPLEMENTAL VOCABULARY 16:
AT THE OFFICE

office	о́фис (m.)
desk	стол (m.)
computer	компью́тер (m.)
telephone	телефо́н (m.)

fax machine	факс (m.)
book shelf	книжная полка (f.)
file cabinet	ящик (m.) для картотеки, картотека (f.)
file	папка (f.)
boss	начальник (m.)
colleague	коллега (m.), коллега (f.)
employee	работник (m.), работница (f.), сотрудник (m.), сотрудница (f.)
staff	штат (m.)
company	фирма (f.), компания (f.)
business	бизнес (m.), дело (n.), дела (nom., pl.)
factory	фабрика (f.), завод (m.)
meeting room	комната (f.) для совещаний, переговоров
meeting	совещание (n.), переговоры (pl.)
appointment	приём (m.), встреча (f.)
salary	зарплата (f.)
job	работа (f.), профессия (f.), задание (n.)
busy	занятый
to work	работать
to earn	зарабатывать - заработать

SUPPLEMENTAL VOCABULARY 17: JOBS

police man/woman	милиционер (m./f.)
lawyer	адвокат (m./f.)
doctor	врач (m./f.)
engineer	инженер (m./f.)
businessman/woman	бизнесмен (m./f.)
salesman/woman	продавец (m.)/ продавщица (f.)
teacher	учитель (m.), учительница (f.)
professor	профессор (m./f.), профессора (nom., pl.)
banker	банкир (m./f.)
architect	архитектор (m./f.)
veterinarian	ветеринар (m./f.)
dentist	стоматолог (m./f.)/ зубной врач (m./f.)
stay-at-home mom	домохозяйка (f.)
carpenter	плотник (m./f.)
construction worker	строитель (m./f.)
taxi driver	таксист (m./f.)
artist	художник (m.)/ художница (f.)
writer	писатель (m./f.)/ писательница (f.) (less common; the male term is often preferred to denote female writers)
poet	поэт (m./f.)/поэтесса (f.) (less common; the male term is often preferred to denote female poets)

plumber	водопроводчик (m./f.)/ слесарь-сантехник (m./f.)
electrician	электрик (m./f.)
journalist	журналист (m.)/ журналистка (f.)
actor/actress	актёр (m.)/актриса (f.)
musician	музыкант (m./f.)
farmer	фермер (m.)
secretary/assistant	секретарь (m./f.)/ секретарша (f.) (coll.), ассистент (m./f.)
unemployed	безработный (m.)/ безработная (f.)
retired	пенсионер (m./f.)/ пенсионерка (f.) (coll.)
full-time	полная занятость (f.)
part-time	временная работа (f.)
steady job	постоянная работа (f.)
summer job	работа на лето, летняя работа

B.   At The Museum

I. Nina asks the way to the Hermitage:

Нина: **Извини́те, пожа́луйста. Как дойти́ до Эрмита́жа?**
Nina: Excuse me, how can I get to the Hermitage?

Прохо́жий: **Да э́то недалеко́ отсю́да. Иди́те пря́мо, и музе́й бу́дет сле́ва от вас.**
Passer-by: It's not far from here. Go straight ahead, and the museum will be on the left.

Нина: **Спаси́бо. Мо́жно дойти́ пешко́м?**
Nina: Thanks. So I can walk there?

Прохо́жий: **Да, коне́чно! Жела́ю вам прия́тно провести́ вре́мя в Петербу́рге.**
Passer-by: Yes, of course! Have a pleasant stay in St. Petersburg.

II. Nina goes to the Hermitage with her friend Ivan:

Нина: **Зна́ете, я о́чень интересу́юсь ру́сским иску́сством.**
Nina: You know, I'm very interested in Russian art.

Ива́н: **Я то́же! Я интересу́юсь анти́чным и средневеко́вым иску́сством.**
Ivan: Me too! I'm interested in ancient and medieval art.

Како́й ваш люби́мый пери́од?
What period do you like the best?

Нина: **Я обожа́ю передви́жников! Смотри́те! Вот карти́на худо́жника-передви́жника. Кто её написа́л?**
Nina: I love the Wanderers (*the Peredvizhniki*)! Look! There's a picture by one of the Wandering painters! Who painted it?

Ива́н: **Э́то карти́на Ре́пина.**
Ivan: That's by Repin.

Нина: **Да, ве́рно. В како́м году́ он её написа́л?**
Nina: Oh, yes. What year did he complete it?

Ива́н: **Одну́ мину́точку. Я посмотрю́ . . . В ты́сяча восемьсо́т во́семьдесят четвёртом году́.**
Ivan: Just a moment. I'll look . . . in 1884.

LESSON 40

A. PROBLEMS OF THE PLANET

Проблémы планéты.

Необдýманные индустриáльные проéкты чáсто ведýт к нарушéнию экологи́ческого балáнса на землé. Поэ́тому за послéдние нéсколько лет всё бóльше людéй в ми́ре начинáют выступáть за охрáну приро́ды.

Большýю тревóгу вызывáет потеплéние кли́мата. Учёные покá не мóгут назвáть тóчной причи́ны потеплéния земнóго кли́мата. Мóжет быть, э́то свя́зано с разрушéнием озóнового слóя атмосфéры. Э́то происхóдит, когдá фреóны и други́е синтети́ческие вещества́, содержáщие хлор, поступáют в атмосфéру.

Рýсские специали́сты нашли́ замéну фреóну: соединéние пропáна и бутáна, безврéдное для атмосфéрного слóя. Крóме тогó, плани́руется пóлное прекращéние вы́пуска фреóнов росси́йской хими́ческой промы́шленностью. Росси́я принимáет серьёзные мéры для разрешéния проблéмы разрýшения озóнового слóя.

Обы́чные лю́ди тóже мóгут помóчь в э́том дéле. Для э́того нýжно прекрати́ть пóльзоваться космéтикой, в котóрой распыли́телем слýжат фреóны, рéже включáть кондиционéр и покупáть кáчественные холоди́льники. Мы все должны́ учáствовать в охрáне приро́ды.

Thoughtless industrial projects often lead to the disturbance of the ecological balance on earth. Therefore, in recent years, more and more people in the world have begun to speak out in support of protecting nature.

Warming of the climate (global warming) causes great alarm. Scientists cannot yet name the exact reason for the warming of the earth's climate. Perhaps it is related to the destruction of the ozone layer in the atmosphere. This happens when Freons and other synthetic compounds containing chlorine enter the atmosphere.

Russian specialists found a substitute for Freons—a compound of propane and butane, which is harmless to the atmospheric layer. Moreover, a complete halt in the production of Freons by the Russian chemical industry is being planned. Russia is taking serious measures to solve the problem of the destruction of the ozone layer.

Ordinary people can also help in this matter. For example, it is necessary to stop using cosmetic products in which Freons are propellants, to turn air-conditioning on less often, and to buy refrigerators of good quality. We should all participate in the protection of nature.

SUPPLEMENTAL VOCABULARY 18: NATURE

tree	дерево (n.), деревья (nom., pl.), деревьев (gen., pl.)
flower	цветок (m.), цветы (nom., pl.), цветов (gen., pl.)
forest	лес (m.), леса (nom., pl.)
mountain	гора (f.)
field	поле (n.), поля (nom., pl.), полей (gen., pl.)

river	река (f.)
lake	озеро (n.), озёра (nom., pl.), озёр (gen., pl.)
ocean	океан (m.)
sea	море (n.), моря (nom., pl.), морей (gen., pl.)
beach	пляж (m.)
desert	пустыня (f.)
rock	скала (f.)
sand	песок (m.), пески (nom., pl.)
sky	небо (n.), небеса (nom., pl.)
sun	солнце (n.)
moon	луна (f.)
star	звезда (f.)
water	вода (f.)
land	земля (f.)
plant	растение (n.)
hill	гора (f.), холм (m.)
pond	пруд (m.)

B. PARTICIPLES AND GERUNDS

Participles and gerunds are very important parts of the Russian language, so it is necessary to know how to recognize and to understand them. However, it should be made clear that they are not used very much in simple conversation, but rather in literature and scientific writing.

Participles are verbal adjectives; gerunds are verbal adverbs. Participles are adjectives made out of verbs. The difference between an adjective and a participle is that a participle retains the verbal qualities of tense, aspect, and voice. In every other respect they are adjectives. They have three genders: masculine, feminine, and neuter. They decline like adjectives and agree with the words they modify in gender, case, and number.

	PRESENT PARTICIPLE	PAST PARTICIPLE
говори́ть	говоря́щий, -ая, -ее, -ие	говори́вший, -ая -ее, -ие

PREPOSITIONAL PLURAL:

Мы говори́м о говоря́щих по-англи́йски ученика́х.
We are talking about students who speak English.

Gerunds are verbal adverbs and as such do not change, but can be imperfective or perfective. The imperfectives are characterized by a simultaneous action in any tense. The perfectives are used when there are two actions, one following the other; when the first action is completed, the second one starts.

IMPERFECTIVE
чита́ть

Чита́я, он улыба́лся.
While reading, he was smiling. (The two actions are simultaneous.)

PERFECTIVE
прочита́ть

Прочита́в газе́ту, он встал и ушёл.
Having finished reading the paper, he got up and went away. (One action follows the other in the past or future.)

FINAL REVIEW QUIZ

1. Я хочу́ хорошо́ _____ по-ру́сски. I want to speak Russian well.
2. Кто _____ э́то? Who said that?
3. _____ вы хоти́те ви́деть? Whom do you wish to see?
4. _____ вы да́ли мою́ кни́гу? Whom did you give my book to?
5. С _____ вы бы́ли в теа́тре вчера́? Whom were you with in the theatre yesterday?
6. Э́то всё, _____ он сказа́л. That's all that he said.
7. Для _____ э́то? What's this for?
8. На _____ вы сиди́те? What are you sitting on?
9. У _____ нет карандаша́. I don't have a pencil.
10. О _____ вы говори́ли? Whom were you talking about?
11. У _____ есть ка́рта Москвы́? Do you have a map of Moscow?
12. Вот _____ магази́н. Here's a good store.
13. Я _____ пить. I want a [to] drink.
14. У _____ есть всё. They have everything.
15. _____ удивля́етесь? What are you surprised at?
16. У _____ нет бра́та. She has no brother.
17. Мне _____ пить. I'm thirsty. [I feel like drinking.]
18. Я _____ по-ру́сски. I speak Russian.
19. Мы _____ чита́ть. We want to read.
20. Они́ _____ хорошо́. They understand well.
21. Вы говори́те сли́шком _____. You speak too fast.
22. Пожа́луйста, говори́те _____. Please speak slower.
23. _____ я понима́ю. Now I understand.
24. _____ вре́мени? What time is it?
25. Он _____ домо́й. He goes home (on foot).
26. Мы _____ обе́дать до́ма. We will have dinner at home.
27. Как вас _____ ? What is your name?
28. Как _____ э́тот го́род? What is the name of this city?
29. Спаси́бо, я _____ не хочу́. Thank you, I don't want any more.
30. _____ сего́дня число́? What is today's date?
31. Мне о́чень _____ э́та кни́га. I like this book very much.
32. Он _____ весь ве́чер. He spoke all evening.
33. Он _____ всё, что он знал. He said all he knew (perfective).
34. У меня́ до́ма мно́го _____. I have a lot of books at home.
35. Я хочу́ _____ молока́. I want some more milk.

36. Завтра я _____ письмо брату. Tomorrow I will write a letter to my brother.
37. _____ она красивая! How pretty she is!
38. Он встаёт _____ каждый день. He gets up early every day.
39. Она _____ в Москве. She lived in Moscow.
40. Дети _____ по-русски. The children will speak Russian (imperfective).
41. Вчера мы читали _____. We read the paper yesterday.
42. _____ ему, что я буду у него дома завтра. Tell him that I will be at his house tomorrow.
43. _____ войти? May I come in?
44. Он взял книгу и _____. He took the book and left.
45. Он всегда всё _____. He always forgets everything.
46. Здесь _____ курить. No smoking here.
47. Он ничего _____. He knows nothing. [He doesn't know anything.]
48. Он никогда _____ в Москве. He has never been to Moscow.
49. Доктор сказал, что вам _____ курить. The doctor said that you can't smoke.
50. Всё _____, что _____ кончается. All's well that ends well.
51. Я иду на _____. I am going to work.
52. Мой брат работает _____. My brother works at home.
53. Мы живём в _____. We live in town.
54. Он пишет _____. He is writing with a pencil.
55. Я смотрю на _____. I am looking at my brother.
56. Он любит читать _____. He likes to read newspapers.
57. У меня нет _____ _____. I don't have black pencils.
58. Мы говорим о моём _____. We are talking about my friend.
59. У него нет _____. He has no sister.
60. Он пишет письмо _____. He is writing a letter to his wife.

ANSWERS

1. говори́ть
2. сказа́л
3. Кого́
4. Кому́
5. кем
6. что
7. чего́
8. чём
9. меня́
10. ком
11. вас
12. хоро́ший
13. хочу́
14. них
15. Чему́
16. неё
17. хо́чется
18. говорю́
19. хоти́м
20. понима́ют
21. бы́стро
22. ме́дленнее
23. Тепе́рь
24. Ско́лько
25. идёт
26. бу́дем
27. зову́т
28. называ́ется
29. бо́льше
30. Како́е
31. нра́вится
32. говори́л
33. сказа́л
34. книг
35. ещё
36. напишу́
37. Кака́я
38. ра́но
39. жила́
40. бу́дут говори́ть
41. газе́ту
42. Скажи́те
43. Мо́жно
44. ушёл
45. забыва́ет
46. нельзя́
47. не зна́ет
48. не́ был
49. нельзя́
50. хорошо́ хорошо́
51. рабо́ту
52. до́ма
53. го́роде
54. карандашо́м
55. бра́та
56. газе́ты
57. чёрных каранда́шей
58. дру́ге
59. сестры́
60. жене́

SUMMARY OF
RUSSIAN GRAMMAR

1. THE RUSSIAN ALPHABET

RUSSIAN LETTER	SCRIPT		NAME
Аа	*А*	*а*	ah
Бб	*Б*	*б*	beh
Вв	*В*	*в*	veh
Гг	*Г*	*г*	geh
Дд	*Д*	*д*	deh
Ее	*Е*	*е*	yeh
Ёё	*Ё*	*ё*	yoh
Жж	*Ж*	*ж*	zheh
Зз	*З*	*з*	zeh
Ии	*И*	*и*	ee
Йй	*Й*	*й*	ee (i short)
Кк	*К*	*к*	kah
Лл	*Л*	*л*	ell
Мм	*М*	*м*	em
Нн	*Н*	*н*	en
Оо	*О*	*о*	oh
Пп	*П*	*п*	peh
Рр	*Р*	*р*	err
Сс	*С*	*с*	ess
Тт	*Т*	*т*	teh
Уу	*У*	*у*	ooh
Фф	*Ф*	*ф*	eff
Хх	*Х*	*х*	khah
Цц	*Ц*	*ц*	tseh
Чч	*Ч*	*ч*	cheh
Шш	*Ш*	*ш*	shah
Щщ	*Щ*	*щ*	shchah
Ыы	*Ы*	*ы*	ih

Ьь	*б*	soft sign
Ъъ	*ъ*	hard sign
Ээ	Э *э*	eh
Юю	Ю *ю*	yoo
Яя	Я *я*	yah

2. PRONUNCIATION

VOWELS

The letter a, when stressed, is pronounced like the English *ah;* when unstressed before a stressed syllable, a is pronounced *ah,* but shorter, and in most other positions is given a neuter sound.

The letter o, when stressed, is pronounced *oh;* when unstressed in first place before the stressed syllable or used initially, o is pronounced *ah,* and in all other positions has a neuter sound.

The letter y is pronounced both stressed and unstressed like the English *ooh.*

The letter ы is pronounced somewhat like the *iy* sound in *buoy.*

The letter э is pronounced like the *eh* in *echo.*

Five vowels—е, ё, и, ю, я—have a glide (the sound similar to the final sound in the English word "may") in front of them. The function of these vowels is the palatalization of the preceding consonant, to which they lose the above-mentioned glide. However, when they follow a vowel or a soft or hard sign, or when they appear in the initial position of a word, they are pronounced as in the alphabet—i.e., with an initial glide.

The letter и always palatalizes the preceding consonant and is pronounced like the *ee* in *beet,* except when it follows the letters ж, ц, ш, which are never palatalized, when it is pronounced like the Russian sound ы.

The letter й is never stressed. It is pronounced like the final sound in *boy*.

The letter e always palatalizes the consonant that precedes it, except when that consonant is ж, ц, ш. When stressed, it is pronounced like the *yeh* in *yet;* in unstressed positions it is pronounced like the *eh* in *bet*. Initially, it is pronounced with the glide: stressed, like *yeh;* unstressed, like *yeeh*.

The letter ё always palatalizes the preceding consonant, and is always stressed. It is pronounced *yoh* as in *y'all*.

The letter я always palatalizes the preceding consonant; when stressed, it is pronounced *yah;* when unstressed, it is pronounced like a shortened *ee*. Initially, it retains its glide; when stressed, it is pronounced *yah,* unstressed, yeeh.

The letter ю always palatalizes the preceding consonant. It is pronounced *ooh* in the body of the word; initially it retains its glide and is pronounced *yooh*.

The letter ь is called the "soft" sign; it palatalizes the preceding consonant, allowing the following vowel to retain its glide.

The letter ъ is called the "hard" sign. It indicates that the preceding consonant remains hard and that the following vowel retains its glide.

CONSONANTS

As in every language, Russian consonants may be voiced or voiceless. The pairs are:

RUSSIAN	ENGLISH	
б в г д ж з	(voiced)	b v g d zh z
п ф к т ш с	(voiceless)	p f k t sh s

When two consonants are pronounced together, they must both be either voiced or voiceless. In

Russian, the second one always remains as it is, and the first one changes accordingly:

всё, все, вчера́;   в = v; pronounced *f*

сде́лать, сдать;   с = s; pronounced *z*

The preposition в (in) is very often pronounced *f*:

в шко́ле is pronounced *fshkoh - leh.*

All consonants are voiceless at the end of a word. All consonants can also be hard or soft (i.e., palatalized or nonpalatalized) when followed by the letters е, ё, и, ю, я or ь. Only the consonants ж, ц, and ш are always hard.

3. GENDER

All Russian nouns, pronouns, adjectives, and ordinal numerals, as well as cardinal numerals and even several verb forms have gender: masculine, feminine, or neuter. In the plural there is only one form for all genders.

MASCULINE	FEMININE	NEUTER	PLURAL

Most nouns and pronouns and the past tense of verbs end in:

MASCULINE	FEMININE	NEUTER	PLURAL
hard consonant	а, я	о, е	а, ы, и

Most adjectives, ordinal numerals, and participles end in:

MASCULINE	FEMININE	NEUTER	PLURAL
ой, ый, ий	ая, яя	ое, ее	ые, ие

NOTE
Pronouns, adjectives, and ordinal numerals always agree in gender
with the nouns they modify or represent.

4. CASES

a. With few exceptions, all nouns, pronouns, and
   adjectives decline. Each declension has six cases:

Nominative:	Кто? Что?	Who? What?
Genitive:	Кого? Чего?	Whom? What?
	От кого? От чего?	From whom? From what?
	У кого? У чего?	At or by whom/what?
	Без кого? Без чего?	Without whom/what?
Dative:	Кому? Чему?	To whom? To what?
	К кому? К чему?	Toward whom/what?
Accusative:	Кого? Что?	Whom? What?
	Куда?	Where (direction toward)?
Instrumental:	Кем? Чем?	By whom? By what?
	С кем? С чем?	With whom? With what?
Prepositional	О ком? О чём?	About whom/what?
or Locative:	В ком? В чём?	In whom? In what?
	Где?	Where (location)?

b. Overall characteristics of the cases and most
   used prepositions:

1. The nominative case supplies the subject of
   the sentence.

2. The genitive case is the case of possession
   and negation. It is also used with many prepositions, the most common of which are:

без	without
для	for
до	up to
из	out of
óколо	near

от	from
после	after
у	at or by

3. The dative case is used in the meaning of "to whom." Prepositions governing the dative case are:

к	to
по	along

4. The accusative is the direct object case. Prepositions used with this case include:

в	to, into
за	behind (direction)
на	to, into, on (direction)

5. The instrumental case indicates the manner of action or instrument with which the action is performed. Prepositions governing the instrumental case include:

между	between
перед	in front of
над	over
под	under (location)
за	behind (location)

6. The prepositional or locative case indicates location and is also used when speaking about something or someone. The prepositions most frequently used with this case are:

в	in
на	on
о	about
при	in the presence of

5. DECLENSION OF NOUNS

	MASCULINE SINGULAR			
	HARD		SOFT	
	ANIMATE	INANIMATE	ANIMATE	INANIMATE
	STUDENT	QUESTION	INHABITANT	SHED
Nom.	студе́нт	вопро́с	жи́тель	сара́й
Gen.	студе́нт-а	вопро́с-а	жи́тел-я	сара́-я
Dat.	студе́нт-у	вопро́с-у	жи́тел-ю	сара́-ю
Acc.	студе́нт-а	вопро́с	жи́тел-я	сара́й
Inst.	студе́нт-ом	вопро́с-ом	жи́тел-ем	сара́-ем
Prep.	о студе́нт-е	о вопро́с-е	о жи́тел-е	о сара́-е

	MASCULINE PLURAL			
Nom.	студе́нт-ы	вопро́с-ы	жи́тел-и	сара́-и
Gen.	студе́нт-ов	вопро́с-ов	жи́тел-ей	сара́-ев
Dat.	студе́нт-ам	вопро́с-ам	жи́тел-ям	сара́-ям
Acc.	студе́нт-ов	вопро́с-ы	жи́тел-ей	сара́-и
Inst.	студе́нт-ами	вопро́с-ами	жи́тел-ями	сара́-ями
Prep.	о студе́нт-ах	о вопро́с-ах	о жи́тел-ях	о сара́-ях

NOTE

The accusative case of animate masculine nouns is the same as the genitive, while the accusative of inanimate masculine nouns is the same as the nominative.

FEMININE SINGULAR		
HARD	SOFT	
ROOM	EARTH	FAMILY

Nom.	ко́мната	земля́	семья́
Gen.	ко́мнат-ы	земл-и́	семь-и́
Dat.	ко́мнат-е	земл-е́	семь-е́
Acc.	ко́мнат-у	зе́мл-ю	семь-ю́
Inst.	ко́мнат-ой(-ою)[1]	земл-ёй(-ёю)	семь-ёй(-ёю)
Prep.	о ко́мнат-е	о земл-е́	о семь-е́

FEMININE PLURAL		

Nom.	ко́мнат-ы	зе́мл-и	се́мь-и
Gen.	ко́мнат	земе́л-ь	сем-е́й
Dat.	ко́мнат-ам	зе́мл-ям	се́мь-ям
Acc.	ко́мнат-ы	зе́мл-и	се́мь-и
Inst.	ко́мнат-ами	зе́мл-ями	се́мь-ями
Prep.	о ко́мнат-ах	о зе́мл-ях	о се́мь-ях

NEUTER SINGULAR		
HARD	SOFT	
WINDOW	SEA	WISH

Nom.	окно́	мо́ре	жела́ние
Gen.	окн-а́	мо́р-я	жела́н-ия
Dat.	окн-у́	мо́р-ю	жела́н-ию
Acc.	окн-о́	мо́р-е	жела́н-ие
Inst.	окн-о́м	мо́р-ем	жела́н-ием
Prep.	об[2] окн-е́	о мо́р-е	о жела́н-ии

NEUTER PLURAL		

Nom.	о́кн-а	мор-я́	жела́н-ия
Gen.	о́к-он	мор-е́й	жела́н-ий
Dat.	о́кн-ам	мор-я́м	жела́н-иям
Acc.	о́кн-а	мор-я́	жела́н-ия
Inst.	о́кн-ами	мор-я́ми	жела́н-иями
Prep.	об[1] о́кн-ах	о мор-я́х	о жела́н-иях

[1] This variant is poetic or dialectal.
[2] **б** is added to the preposition here for the sake of euphony.

SOME IRREGULAR DECLENSIONS

	SINGULAR			
	MASC.	FEMININE		NEUTER
	ROAD	MOTHER	DAUGHTER	NAME
Nom.	путь	мать	дочь	и́мя
Gen.	пут-и́	ма́т-ери	до́ч-ери	и́м-ени
Dat.	пут-и́	ма́т-ери	до́ч-ери	и́м-ени
Acc.	путь	мать	дочь	и́мя
Inst.	пут-ём	ма́т-ерью	до́ч-ерью	и́м-енем
Prep.	о пут-и́	о ма́т-ери	о до́ч-ери	об и́м-ени

	PLURAL				
Nom.	пут-и́	ма́т-ери	до́ч-ери	им-ена́	де́т-и
Gen.	пут-е́й	мат-ере́й	доч-ере́й	им-ён	дет-е́й
Dat.	пут-я́м	мат-еря́м	доч-еря́м	им-ена́м	де́т-ям
Acc.	пут-и́	мат-ере́й[1]	доч-ере́й	им-ена́	дет-е́й[1]
Inst.	пут-я́ми	мат-еря́ми	доч-еря́ми	им-ена́ми	дет-ьми́
Prep.	о пут-я́х	о мат-еря́х	о доч-еря́х	об им-ена́х	о де́т-ях

6. DECLENSION OF ADJECTIVES

	SINGULAR					
	MASC.	FEM.	NEUT.	MASC.	FEM.	NEUT.
	ый	ая	ое	ой	ая	ое
Nom.	но́вый	но́вая	но́вое	сухо́й	суха́я	сухо́е
Gen.	но́в-ого	но́в-ой	но́в-ого	сух-о́го	сух-о́й	сух-о́го
Dat.	но́в-ому	но́в-ой	но́в-ому	сух-о́му	сух-о́й	сух-о́му
Acc.	Same as nom. or gen.	но́в-ую	но́в-ое	Same as nom. or gen.	сух-у́ю	сух-о́е
Inst.	но́в-ым	но́в-ой(-ою)	но́в-ым	сух-и́м	сух-о́й(-ою)	сух-и́м
Prep.	о но́в-ом	о но́в-ой	о но́в-ом	о сух-о́м	о сухо́й	о сух-о́м

[1] The accusative plural of animate neuter nouns and most feminine nouns is the same as the genitive plural.

	PLURAL	
Nom.	но́в-ые	сух-и́е
Gen.	но́в-ых	сух-и́х
Dat.	но́в-ым	сух-и́м
Acc.	Same as nom. or gen.	Same as nom. or gen.
Inst.	но́в-ыми	сух-и́ми
Prep.	о но́в-ых	о сух-и́х

	SINGULAR			PLURAL
	MASC.	FEM.	NEUT.	
Nom.	си́н-ий	си́н-яя	си́н-ее	си́н-ие
Gen.	си́н-его	си́н-ей	си́н-его	си́н-их
Dat.	си́н-ему	си́н-ей	си́н-ему	си́н-им
Acc.	Same as nom. or gen.	си́н-юю	си́н-ее	Same as nom. or gen.
Inst.	си́н-им	си́н-ей(-ею)	си́н-им	си́н-ими
Prep.	о си́н-ем	о си́н-ей	о си́н-ем	о си́н-их

7. DECLENSION OF PRONOUNS

	SINGULAR				
	1ST PERSON	2ND PERSON	3RD PERSON		
			MASC.	NEUT.	FEM.
Nom.	я	ты	он	оно́	она́
Gen.	меня́	тебя́	его́	его́	её
Dat.	мне́	тебе́	ему́	ему́	ей
Acc.	меня́	тебя́	его́	его́	её
Instr.	мной(-о́ю)	тобо́й(-о́ю)	им	им	ей, е́ю
Prep.	обо мне́	о тебе́	о нём	о нём	о ней

| | PLURAL | | |
	1ST PERSON	2ND PERSON	3RD PERSON
Nom.	мы	вы	они́
Gen.	нас	вас	их
Dat.	нам	вам	им
Acc.	нас	вас	их
Instr.	на́ми	ва́ми	и́ми
Prep.	о нас	о вас	о них

| REFLEXIVE PRONOUN |
SING. OR PLURAL
—
себя́
себе́
себя́
собо́й(-о́ю)
о себе́

| | MY | | | |
| | SINGULAR | | | PLURAL |
	MASC.	FEM.	NEUTER	ALL GENDERS
Nom.	мой	моя́	моё	мои́
Gen.	моего́	мое́й	моего́	мои́х
Dat.	моему́	мое́й	моему́	мои́м
Acc.	Same as nom. or gen.	мою́	моё	Same as nom. or gen.
Inst.	мои́м	мое́й(-е́ю)	мои́м	мои́ми
Prep.	о моём	о мое́й	о моём	о мои́х

твой (your, sing.), свой (one's own, their own) are
declined in the same way.

For the third-person possessive, the genitive case of
the personal pronouns is used. It always agrees with
the gender and number of the possessor.

Nominative	Genitive	
он	его́	his
она́	её	her
оно́	его́	its
они́	их	their

	OUR			
	SINGULAR			PLURAL
	MASC.	FEM.	NEUT.	ALL GENDERS
Nom.	наш	на́ша	на́ше	на́ши
Gen.	на́ш-его	на́ш-ей	на́ш-его	на́ш-их
Dat.	на́ш-ему	на́ш-ей	на́ш-ему	на́ш-им
Acc.	Same as nom or or gen.	на́ш-у	на́ше	Same as nom. or gen.
Inst.	на́ш-им	на́ш-ей(-ею)	на́ш-им	на́ш-ими
Prep.	о на́ш-ем	о на́ш-ей	о на́ш-ем	о на́ш-их

ваш (your, *plural* or *polite*) is declined in the same way.

	ALL			
	SINGULAR			PLURAL
	MASC.	FEM.	NEUT.	ALL GENDERS
Nom.	весь	вся	всё	все
Gen.	вс-его́	вс-ей	вс-его́	вс-ех
Dat.	вс-ему́	вс-ей	вс-ему́	вс-ем
Acc.	Same as nom. or gen.	вс-ю	всё	Same as nom. or gen.
Inst.	вс-ем	вс-ей(-ею)	вс-ем	вс-е́ми
Prep.	обо вс-ём	обо вс-ей	обо вс-ём	обо вс-ех

	SINGULAR THIS			PLURAL THESE
	MASC.	FEM.	NEUT.	ALL GENDERS
Nom.	э́тот	э́та	э́то	э́ти
Gen.	э́т-ого	э́т-ой	э́т-ого	э́т-их
Dat.	э́т-ому	э́т-ой	э́т-ому	э́т-им
Acc.	Same as nom. or gen.	э́т-у	э́то	Same as nom. or gen.
Inst.	э́т-им	э́т-ой	э́т-им	э́т-ими
Prep.	об э́т-ом	об э́т-ой	об э́т-ом	об э́т-их

		SINGULAR THAT		PLURAL THOSE
	MASC.	FEM.	NEUT.	ALL GENDERS
Nom.	тот	та	то	те
Gen.	т-ого́	т-ой	т-ого́	т-ех
Dat.	т-ому́	т-ой	т-ому́	т-ем
Acc.	Same as nom. or gen.	т-у	т-о	Same as nom. or gen.
Inst.	т-ем	т-ой	т-ем	т-е́ми
Prep.	о т-ом	о т-ой	о т-ом	о т-ех

		SINGULAR ONESELF		PLURAL THEMSELVES
	MASC.	FEM.	NEUT.	ALL GENDERS
Nom.	сам	сама́	само́	са́ми
Gen.	сам-ого́	сам-о́й	сам-ого́	сам-и́х
Dat.	сам-ому́	сам-о́й	сам-ому́	сам-и́м
Acc.	Same as nom. or gen.	сам-у́	сам-о́	Same as nom. or gen.
Inst.	сам-и́м	сам-о́й	сам-и́м	сам-и́ми
Prep.	о сам-о́м	о сам-о́й	о сам-о́м	о сам-и́х

		SINGULAR WHOSE		PLURAL
	MASC.	FEM.	NEUT.	ALL GENDERS
Nom.	чей	чья	чьё	чьи
Gen.	чьего́	чьей	чьего́	чьих
Dat.	чьему́	чьей	чьему́	чьим
Acc.	Same as nom. or gen.	чью	чьё	Same as nom. or gen.
Inst.	чьим	чьей	чьим	чьи́ми
Prep.	о чьём	о чьей	о чьём	о чьих

8. COMPARATIVE OF ADJECTIVES

To form the comparative of an adjective, drop the gender ending and add -ee for all genders and the plural, as well. The adjective does not decline in the comparative:

краси́вый	pretty
краси́в-ее	prettier
тёплый	warm
тепл-е́е	warmer
весёлый	merry
весел-е́е	merrier

IRREGULAR COMPARATIVE FORMS

хоро́ший	good
лу́чше	better
большо́й	big
бо́льше	bigger
ма́ленький	small
ме́ньше	smaller
широ́кий	wide
ши́ре	wider
у́зкий	narrow
у́же	narrower
плохо́й	bad
ху́же	worse
высо́кий	tall
вы́ше	taller
ти́хий	quiet
ти́ше	quieter
дорого́й	dear/expensive
доро́же	dearer/more expensive
просто́й	simple
про́ще	simpler
то́лстый	fat
то́лще	fatter

9.   SUPERLATIVE OF ADJECTIVES

The superlative of adjectives has two forms. The simpler form—the one we will discuss here—makes use of the word са́мый, са́мая, са́мое, са́мые (the most):

са́мый большо́й	the biggest
са́мая краси́вая	the prettiest
са́мый у́мный	the most clever

The word са́мый declines with the adjective:

в са́мом большо́м до́ме
in the very largest house

Он пришёл с са́мой краси́вой же́нщиной.
He came with the prettiest woman.

10.   CASES USED WITH CARDINAL NUMERALS

оди́н (*m.*), одна́ (*f.*), одно́ (*n.*), одни́ (*pl.*)
два (*m.*), две (*f.*), два (*n.*)

A. When the number is used in the nominative case:

after оди́н, одна́, одно́—use the nominative *singular*.
after одни́—use the nominative *plural*.
after два, две, три, четы́ре—use the genitive *singular*.
after пять, шесть, семь, etc.—use the genitive *plural*.

B. When the number is compound, the case of the noun depends on the last digit:

два́дцать оди́н каранда́ш (nominative *singular*)
twenty-one pencils

два́дцать два карандаша́ (genitive *singular*)
twenty-two pencils
два́дцать пять карандаше́й (genitive *plural*)
twenty-five pencils

11. DECLENSION OF CARDINAL NUMERALS

All cardinal numerals decline, agreeing in case with
the noun they modify (with the exception of the nominative and the accusative cases, discussed above).

Я оста́лся без одно́й копе́йки. (genitive *singular*)
I was left without one cent.

Он был там оди́н ме́сяц без двух дней. (genitive
    plural)
He was there one month less two days.

Мы пришли́ к пяти́ часа́м. (dative *plural*)
We arrived about five o'clock.

Они́ говоря́т о семи́ кни́гах. (prepositional *plural*)
They are speaking about seven books.

DECLENSION OF NUMERALS

	SINGULAR ONE			PLURAL ONLY
	MASC.	FEM.	NEUT.	(ALL GENDERS)
Nom.	оди́н	одна́	одно́	одни́
Gen.	одного́	одно́й	одного́	одни́х
Dat.	одному́	одно́й	одному́	одни́м
Acc.	Same as nom. or gen.	одну́	одно́	Same as nom. or gen.
Inst.	одни́м	одно́й(-о́ю)	одни́м	одни́ми
Prep.	об одно́м	об одно́й	об одно́м	об одни́х

	TWO	THREE	FOUR	FIVE
Nom.	два, две	три	четы́ре	пять
Gen.	двух	трёх	четырёх	пяти́
Dat.	двум	трём	четырём	пяти́
Acc.	Same as nom. or gen.	Same as nom. or gen.	Same as nom. or gen.	пять
Inst.	двумя́	тремя́	четырьмя́	пятью́
Prep.	о двух	о трёх	о четырёх	о пяти́

NOTE
All numbers from 6 to 20 follow the same declension pattern as 5.

12. ORDINAL NUMERALS

All ordinal numerals are like adjectives, and decline in the same way as adjectives:

MASC.	FEM.	NEUT.	PLURAL (ALL GENDERS)
пе́рвый	пе́рвая	пе́рвое	пе́рвые
второ́й	втора́я	второ́е	вторы́е

When they are compound, only the last digit changes its form, and only that digit is declined.

двадца́тый век   twentieth century

Это бы́ло три́дцать пе́рвого декабря́.	That was on December 31.
тре́тий раз	third time
Втора́я мирова́я война́ ко́нчилась в ты́сяча девятьсо́т со́рок пя́том году́.	The Second World War ended in 1945 (one thousand, nine hundred, forty-fifth year).
пя́тый год (в) пя́том году́	(prepositional singular)

13. DOUBLE NEGATIVES

With words such as:

ничего́	nothing
никто́	nobody
никогда́	never
никуда́	nowhere

a second negative must be used:

I nothing	don't	(verb)
Я ничего́	не	хочу́, зна́ю.

Nobody	don't	(verb)
Никто́	не	ви́дит, говори́т.

Never	don't	(verb)
Он никогда́	не	был в Москве́.
Мы никогда́	не	говори́м по-ру́сски.

A negative adverb or pronoun must use a negative with the verb it modifies. (For more on negative expressions, see pages 97–98.)

14. VERBS

Russian verbs have two conjugations. Infinitives of most verbs belonging to the first conjugation end with -ать or -ять. Infinitives of verbs belonging to the second conjugation end with -еть or -ить. Although this is true of a great body of Russian verbs, there are many exceptions, several of which are included in this summary.

A. TYPICAL CONJUGATIONS OF IMPERFECTIVE VERBS:

FIRST CONJUGATION
читáть   to read

Present Tense:

я читáю
ты читáешь
он читáет
мы читáем
вы читáете
они́ читáют

Past Tense:

читáл (*m.*)
читáла (*f.*)
читáло (*n.*)
читáли (*pl.*)

Future Tense:

я бу́ду
ты бу́дешь
он бу́дет
мы бу́дем   } читáть
вы бу́дете
они́ бу́дут

Conditional:

читáл бы
читáла бы

читáло бы
читáли бы

Imperative: читáй
                       читáйте

Participles:

Active:
Present Tense: читáющий
Past Tense: читáвший

Passive:
Present Tense: читáемый

Gerund:
Present Tense: читáя

SECOND CONJUGATION
говори́ть   to speak

Present Tense: я говорю́
                       ты говори́шь
                       он говори́т
                       мы говори́м
                       вы говори́те
                       они́ говоря́т

Past Tense: говори́л (*m.*)
                       говори́ла (*f.*)
                       говори́ло (*n.*)
                       говори́ли (*pl.*)

Future Tense:	я бу́ду
	ты бу́дешь
	он бу́дет
	мы бу́дем } говори́ть
	вы бу́дете
	они́ бу́дут

Conditional:	говори́л бы
	говори́ла бы
	говори́ло бы
	говори́ли бы

| Imperative: | говори́ |
| | говори́те |

Participles:

| Present Tense: | говоря́щий |
| Past Tense: | говори́вший |

Gerund:

| Present Tense: | говоря́ |

B. MIXED CONJUGATION — PRESENT TENSE

хоте́ть TO WANT	
я хочу́	мы хоти́м
ты хо́чешь	вы хоти́те
он хо́чет	они́ хотя́т

NOTE
This verb in the singular has first conjugation endings, with the т

changing to ч. In the plural it has second-conjugation endings. The
past tense is regular.

C. REFLEXIVE VERBS:

Verbs ending with -ся or -сь are reflexive (-ся usually
follows a consonant, and -сь a vowel). These verbs
follow the general form of conjugation, retaining the
endings -ся after consonants and -сь after vowels.

ЗАНИМА́ТЬСЯ	
TO STUDY	
я занима́юсь	мы занима́емся
ты занима́ешься	вы занима́етесь
он занима́ется	они́ занима́ются

D. THE VERB "TO BE"

The verb "to be" (быть) is usually omitted in the
present tense, but is used in the past tense:

был (*m.*)
была́ (*f.*)
бы́ло (*n.*)
бы́ли (*pl.*)

and in the future tense:

я бу́ду   мы бу́дем
ты бу́дешь   вы бу́дете
он бу́дет   они́ бу́дут

It is also used as an auxiliary verb in the imperfective future.

E. Conjugations of Some Irregular Verbs in the Present Tense

брать то таке	
я беру́	мы берём
ты берёшь	вы берёте
он берёт	они́ беру́т

вести́ то LEAD	
я веду́	мы ведём
ты ведёшь	вы ведёте
он ведёт	они́ веду́т

жить то LIVE	
я живу́	мы живём
ты живёшь	вы живёте
он живёт	они́ живу́т

звать то CALL	
я зову́	мы зовём
ты зовёшь	вы зовёте
он зовёт	они́ зову́т

нести́ то CARRY	
я несу́	мы несём
ты несёшь	вы несёте
он несёт	они́ несу́т

дава́ть то GIVE	
я даю́	мы даём
ты даёшь	вы даёте
он даёт	они́ даю́т

F. Conjugations of Irregular Perfective Verbs — Perfective Future

ДАТЬ TO GIVE	
я дам	мы дади́м
ты дашь	вы дади́те
он даст	они́ даду́т

СЕСТЬ TO SIT DOWN	
я ся́ду	мы ся́дем
ты ся́дешь	вы ся́дете
он ся́дет	они́ ся́дут

G. Perfective and Imperfective Aspects of a Verb

Russian verbs can be perfective or imperfective. Imperfective verbs express continuous action. They have three tenses: past, present, and future. Perfective verbs indicate completion of action, beginning of action, or both, and have only two tenses: past and future.

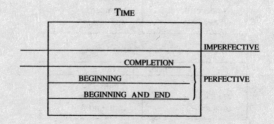

Some perfective verbs are formed by adding the prefixes с, на, вы, в, по, etc., to imperfective verbs. When a prefix is added to a verb, not only is the perfective formed, but very often the meaning of the verb is changed at the same time.

IMPERFECTIVE	PERFECTIVE
писа́ть to write	написа́ть to write down, to finish writing
	переписа́ть to copy

When the meaning of the verb changes, the new verb переписа́ть (to copy) that has been formed must have its own imperfective. To form the imperfective of such new forms, the suffix -ыв, -ив, or -ав is added:

IMPERFECTIVE	PERFECTIVE	IMPERFECTIVE
писа́ть (to write)	переписа́ть (to copy)	перепи́сывать
чита́ть (to read)	прочита́ть (to finish reading or to read through)	прочи́тывать
	перечита́ть (to read over)	перечи́тывать
знать (to know)	узна́ть (to find out or to recognize)	узнава́ть
дава́ть (to give)	дать	
	отда́ть (to give out or away)	отдава́ть
	переда́ть (to pass)	передава́ть
	зада́ть (to assign)	задава́ть
	сдать (to deal cards)	сдава́ть

Some perfective verbs have different roots:

говори́ть (to speak)	сказа́ть (to tell)	
	заговори́ть (to begin talking)	загова́ривать

рассказа́ть	расска́зывать
(to tell a story)	
заказа́ть	зака́зывать
(to order something	
to be made or done)	
приказа́ть	прика́зывать
(to order, to command)	

Prefixes can be added to either говори́ть or сказа́ть, but each addition makes a new verb, e.g.:

за-говори́ть	to begin talking
за-каза́ть	to order something
от-говори́ть	to talk someone out of something
(от-гова́ривать)	
рассказа́ть	to tell a story

The past tense of the perfective verb is formed in the same way as the past tense of the imperfective verb.

H. Future Tense

The future tense has two forms: imperfective future and perfective future. As has already been pointed out, the imperfective future is formed by using the auxiliary verb быть, with the infinitive of the imperfective verb:

я бу́ду		I will	
ты бу́дешь		you will	
он бу́дет	говори́ть, чита́ть,	he will	speak, read,
мы бу́дем	понима́ть, etc.	we will	understand, etc.
вы бу́дете		you will	
они́ бу́дут		they will	

The perfective future is formed without using the auxiliary verb быть:

Present		Perfective Future	
Я пишу́	I write	я напишу́	I will write
ты говори́шь	you speak	ты ска́жешь	you will say
он идёт	he goes	он придёт	he will come
мы чита́ем	we read	мы прочита́ем	we will read (it)

Present		Perfective Future	
вы смо́трите	you look	вы посмо́трите	you will look
они́ е́дут	they go [ride]	они́ прие́дут	they will come [riding]

NOTE

The perfective verb is conjugated in the same way as the imperfective verb.

I.   VERBS OF MOTION

Verbs of motion have many variations of meaning. A different verb is used to express movement by a conveyance than is used to express movement by foot.

Each of these verbs (i.e., indicating movement by foot or movement by conveyance) has two forms: one describes a single action in one direction, and the other, a repeated action. All of these forms are imperfective. The perfective is formed by adding a prefix to a single-action verb. But bear in mind that the addition of the prefix changes the meaning of the verb. The same prefix affixed to the repeated-action verb forms the imperfective of the new verb.

IMPERFECTIVE	REPEATED ACTION		ONE ACTION	PERFECTIVE
выходить выезжать приходить приезжать заходить заезжать	ходить ездить	to go on foot to go by vehicle to go out on foot to go out by vehicle to come on foot [arrive] to come by vehicle [arrive] to drop in [visit] on foot to drop in [visit] by vehicle	идти ехать	выйти выехать прийти приехать зайти заехать
приносить привозить	носить возить	to carry on foot to carry by vehicle to bring on foot to bring by vehicle	нести везти	принести привезти

ИДТИ́	
TO GO ON FOOT	
(SINGLE ACTION IN ONE DIRECTION)	
PRESENT TENSE	PAST TENSE
я иду́ ты идёшь он идёт мы идём вы идёте они́ иду́т	он шёл она́ шла оно́ шло они́ шли

ХОДИ́ТЬ	
TO GO ON FOOT	
(REPEATED ACTION)	
PRESENT TENSE	PAST TENSE
я хожу́ ты хо́дишь он хо́дит мы хо́дим вы хо́дите они́ хо́дят	Regular

Е́ХАТЬ	
TO GO BY VEHICLE	
(SINGLE ACTION IN ONE DIRECTION)	
PRESENT TENSE	PAST TENSE
я е́ду ты е́дешь он е́дет мы е́дем вы е́дете они́ е́дут	Regular

ездить	
TO GO BY VEHICLE	
(REPEATED ACTION)	
PRESENT TENSE	PAST TENSE
я езжу ты ездишь он ездит мы ездим вы ездите они ездят	Regular

нести́	
TO CARRY ON FOOT	
(SINGLE ACTION IN ONE DIRECTION)	
PRESENT TENSE	PAST TENSE
я несу́ ты несёшь он несёт мы несём вы несёте они несу́т	он нёс она несла́ оно несло́ они несли́

носи́ть	
TO CARRY ON FOOT	
(REPEATED ACTION)	
PRESENT TENSE	PAST TENSE
я ношу́ ты но́сишь он но́сит мы но́сим вы но́сите они но́сят	Regular

ВЕЗТИ́	
TO CARRY BY VEHICLE	
(SINGLE ACTION IN ONE DIRECTION)	
Present Tense	Past Tense
я везу́	
ты везёшь	
он везёт	он вёз
мы везём	она́ везла́
вы везёте	оно́ везло́
они́ везу́т	они́ везли́

ВОЗИ́ТЬ	
TO CARRY BY VEHICLE	
(REPEATED ACTION)	
Present Tense	Past Tense
я вожу́	Regular
ты во́зишь	
он во́зит	
мы во́зим	
вы во́зите	
они́ во́зят	

J. Subjunctive and Conditional Moods

The subjunctive and conditional in many languages constitute one of the most difficult grammatical constructions. However, in Russian they are the easiest. To form the subjunctive or conditional, the past tense of the verb is used together with the particle бы:

е́сли бы   if

Е́сли бы я знал }   If I knew,
                      Had I known,

Я пошёл бы.}	I would have gone. I would go.

Я позвони́л бы,
  е́сли бы у меня́
  был ваш но́мер.
	I would have called you,
	  if I had your tele-
	  phone number.

K. IMPERATIVE MOOD

The imperative mood of a verb (see page 171) is formed from the second-person singular, present tense. For the singular imperative, replace the ending with -и, -й, or -ь. If the ending has two consonants, add an -и regardless of the stress. For the plural imperative, add -те to the singular:

INFINITIVE	SECOND-PERSON SINGULAR	FAMILIAR, SINGULAR	POLITE, PLURAL
писа́ть to write	пи́ш-ешь	пиши́!	пиши́те!
повторя́ть to repeat	повторя́-ешь	повторя́й!	повторя́йте!
броса́ть to throw	броса́-ешь	броса́й!	броса́йте!
рабо́тать to work	рабо́та-ешь	рабо́тай!	рабо́тайте!
чита́ть to read	чита́-ешь	чита́й!	чита́йте!
по́мнить to remember	по́мнишь	по́мни!	по́мните!

The reflexive verb retains its endings (-ся after a consonant or -й, and -сь after a vowel):

мы́ться to wash (oneself)	мо́-ешься	мо́йся!	мо́йтесь!
занима́ться to study	занима́ешься	занима́йся!	занима́йтесь!

In giving an order indirectly to a third person, the forms пусть and пуска́й (coll.) are used with the third person singular:

Пусть он чита́ет.	Let him read.	(He should read.)
Пуска́й она́ говори́т.	Let her speak.	(She should speak.)

L. PARTICIPLES AND GERUNDS

Participles and gerunds are very important parts of the Russian language, so it is necessary to know how to recognize them and to understand them. However, it should be made clear that they are not used very much in simple conversation, but rather in literature and scientific writing.

Participles are verb-adjectives; gerunds are verb-adverbs. Participles are adjectives made out of verbs. The difference between an adjective and a participle is that a participle retains the verbal qualities of tense, aspect and voice. In every other respect they are adjectives. They have three genders: masculine, feminine, and neuter. They decline the same as adjectives and agree with the words they modify in gender, case, and number.

	PRESENT	PAST
Говори́ть	говоря́щий, -ая, -ее, -ие	говори́вший, -ая, -ее, -ие

PREPOSITIONAL PLURAL:

Мы говори́м о говоря́щих по-англи́йски ученика́х.
We are talking about students who speak English.

Gerunds are verb-adverbs and as such do not change, but can be imperfective and perfective. The imperfectives are characterized by a simultaneous action in any tense. The perfectives are used when there are two actions, one following the other; when the first action is completed, the second one starts.

Imperfective
читáть

Читáя, он улыбáлся.
While reading, he was smiling
(two simultaneous actions).

Perfective
прочитáть

Прочитáв газéту, он встал и
ушёл.
Having finished reading the
paper, he got up and went
away
(one action following the
other).

LETTER AND E-MAIL WRITING

A. A NOTE ON LETTER WRITING

Both in formal and informal writing, the addressee's name, title, and postal address usually appear only on the envelope. In formal letters, an institution's name and address often appear at the top of the document, while the date is found at the bottom of the page.

Since the demise of the Soviet Union, the form of address in formal writing has changed. Instead of writing to a "comrade" (това́рищ), Russians now write to Mr. or Mrs. (господи́н, госпожа́). The abbreviated forms are г-н (or simply г.) for Mr. and г-жа for Mrs. In formal writing the use of a title is common, and if one wants to write to editorial offices of newspapers or journals, the phrase "Dear editorial board" (Уважа́емая реда́кция) is commonly used.

The abbreviated form of the date differs from the one used in the United States. December 20, 2005, for example, is written as 20-12-05 or as 20/XII/05. Address writing is different as well. Russians begin with the city, then write the street and house number, then apartment number, then the name of the addressee (in dative case).

B. BUSINESS LETTERS

> г. Москва 157332
> Ул. Петрова, д. 8
> Всероссийское издательство «Наука»
> Отдел по международным связям

Уважаемый г. Степанов!

Мы получили Ваш заказ на доставку последних номеров журнала «Континент». К сожалению, в связи с повышением почтовых тарифов, мы не смогли отправить заказ вовремя. Доставка журналов ожидается в первых числах ноября.

С уважением,
Г. И. Аполлонов
Директор отдела по
международным связям

12 октября 2005[1]
г. Москва

> Moskva 157332
> Petrova 8
> All-Russian Publishing House "Science"
> Section on Foreign Affairs

Dear Mr. Stepanov,

We have received your order to deliver the latest issues of the journal *Kontinent*. Unfortunately, due to the increases in postal tariffs, we could not send you your order on time. The delivery of the issues is expected in early November.

> Sincerely,
> G. I. Apollonov
> Director of the Section on
> Foreign Affairs

October 12, 2005
Moscow

[1] The date may also follow the addressee's address.

г. Москва 122771
Ул. Васнецова, д. 2
Совместное предприятие «Роза»

Уважаемый г. Кожинов!

Отвечаем на Ваш запрос о возможности установить
торговые связи с Германией. К сожалению, в настоящее
время мы не в состоянии помочь Вам в этом деле. Наше
предприятие не уполномочено действовать в качестве
посредника между западными и русскими фирмами.

С уважением,
Н. И. Сошников
Директор предприятия

13/XI/05
г. Москва

Moskva 122771
Vasnetsova St. 2
Joint Venture "Rose"

Dear Mr. Kozhinov,

This is in response to your inquiry about the possibility of
establishing trade contacts with Germany. Unfortunately, we are
unable to help you at present. Our business is not authorized to act
as mediators between Western and Russian firms.

Sincerely,
N. I. Soshnikov
Director of the firm

November 13, 2005
Moscow

C. INFORMAL LETTERS

27-10-06

Дорогой Иван!

Наконец, приехал в Псков. С билетами было трудно, но, в конце концов, Ирина достала, и даже на скорый поезд. В общем, могу взяться за работу. Директор нашёл неплохую квартиру. Наверное, действительно хотят, чтобы мне было удобно. Жалко, что не успели поговорить в Москве, но в ноябре собираюсь приехать и, конечно, позвоню.

Скучаю по московским друзьям. Не забывай. Пиши!

Сергей

10-27-06

Dear Ivan,

I have finally arrived in Pskov. There was difficulty with the tickets, but in the end Irina managed to get them and even for an express train. So, I can get down to work. The director found a decent apartment. It seems they really want to make me comfortable. Too bad we didn't have time to talk in Moscow, but I plan to come in November and will call you of course.

I miss my Moscow friends. Don't forget me. Write!

Sergei

17-11-05

Дорогая Наташа!

Давно уже не получаю от тебя писем и очень беспокоюсь о родителях. Как здоровье отца? Собирается мама уходить на пенсию или опять откладывает? Позвони мне на работу, домашний телефон ещё не подключили.
Девочки растут, Марина пошла в первый класс и очень гордится. Таня даёт ей советы.
Все у нас хорошо. Миша передаёт привет. Надеюсь увидеть всех вас на праздники.

Целую,
Ваша Галя

11-17-05

Dear Natasha,

I have not received letters from you in a while and I worry a lot about our parents. How is Father's health? Is Mom going to retire or is she delaying again? Call me at work: our home phone has not yet been connected.
The girls are growing. Marina started first grade and is very proud. Tania gives her advice.
Everything is fine with us. Misha sends regards. I hope to see all of you for the holidays.

Kisses,
Your Galia

D. FORM OF THE ENVELOPE

	addressee
addressee's zip code	sender

1. Business Letters

Куда: г. Москва
ул. Страхова, д.5, кв.75
Кому: Павлову Ивану Петровичу

г. Псков 32435
ул. Надеждина, д.4,кв. 11
332889   Сергей Суриков

Куда: Moscow
Strakhova St. 5, apt.75
Кому: Pavlov, Ivan Petrovich

Pskov 32435
Nadezhdina St. 4, apt. 11
332889   Sergei Surikov

2. Informal Letters

Куда: г. Ставрополь
ул. Кураева, д.1, кв.75
Кому: Семеновой Наталье Ивановне

г. Новосибирск 30897
ул. Королёва, д.15, кв. 33
32456   Г.И. Синицына

Куда: Stavropol 32456
Kuraeva 1, apt.75
Кому: Semenova Natalia Ivanovna

Novosibirsk 30897
Koroleva 15, apt.33
32456   Sinitsina G.I.

The American format of the envelope is becoming
more common now with the sender's name and
address in the upper left corner and the addressee's
name and address in the lower right corner.

От кого **Откуда**	Осокиной Н.Н. ул. Вавиловых д.7 кв.15 г. Санкт-Петербург Россия индекс места отправления **195257**

Кому **Куда**	Петрову А.Г. ул. Обручева д.17 кв.5 г. Москва Россия индекс места отправления **117334**

E. E-MAILS

When Russians write e-mails or create websites, they follow the American format.

Дата:	среда, 9 августа 2004
От кого:	Сидоровская Юлия *sarabumba@mail.ru*
Кому:	Грибовой Натальи *natasha1972@wplus.spb.ru*
Тема:	Ответ на письмо от 29.07.04

Привет, Наташа!

Получила твоё письмо, прочитала его, поменяв кодировку, но, к сожалению, не смогла открыть вложенный файл. Компьютер выдал сообщение, что в нем вирус. Но зато мне удалось открыть ссылку на сайт, которую ты прислала. На этом сайте я нашла всю необходимую информацию. Я также подписалась на рассылку и теперь получаю новости каждый день. Это было не сложно: я зарегистрировалась на сайте, ввела логин и пароль и оставила свой электронный адрес.

Пиши на мой домашний адрес. Жду ответа.

Юля

Date:	Wednesday, August 20, 2004
From Whom:	Сидоровская Юлия *sarabumba@mail.ru*
To Whom:	Грибовой Натальи *natasha1972@wplus.spb.ru*
Subject:	Answer to the letter from 07/29/04

Dear Natasha,

[I] received you letter, read it, having changed the encoding, but unfortunately couldn't open the attached file. The message popped up, that it had a virus. However, I could open the link that you had sent. I found all of the necessary information on that site. I also signed up for the mail list and now I get the news every day. It wasn't hard: I registered on the site, entered my log-in and the password, and typed in [left] my e-mail address.

[Please] write to my personal [e-mail] address. Waiting for your reply,

Julia

In-Flight Russian

Wondering how to make use of all that spare time on the plane while you're flying to Moscow or St. Petersburg? Between your in-flight meal and in-flight movie, brush up on your Russian!

This 60-minute program covers just enough Russian to get by in every travel situation.

CD Program
0-609-81077-4 • $13.95/C$21.00

Ultimate Russian Beginner-Intermediate

Our most comprehensive program for serious language learners, businesspeople, and anyone planning to spend time abroad. This package includes a coursebook and eight 60-minute CDs.

CD Program
1-4000-2117-0 * $79.95/C$110.00

Coursebook Only
1-4000-2116-2 * $18.00/C$26.00